MW00388327

"*Discover Your Inner Goddess Queen* is a treasure chest of precious jewels. Kelly will take you on a journey that is filled with fun and creative ways of bringing out that beautiful, wise, loving, Queen that resides within every woman."

Suzanne Hirabayashi
Author of *An Open & Loving Heart*

"My Goddess Queen is my direct link to God. Getting to know her intimately has brought me faith, courage, trust in myself and others, and an inner knowing that guides me in and out of situations with ease and grace. I am forever grateful to Kelly Sullivan for introducing me to my Goddess Queen."

Jody Sutton
Founding Member of the Goddess Queen Gathering
Sutton Design/Interior Designer

"For all women who are gifted with a desire for self-discovery, Kelly offers a wealth of tools to assist you in awakening to your power and uniting you with your inner Goddess Queen!"

Firestar
Energetic Healer

Discover Your Inner GODDESS QUEEN

An Inspirational Journey
from Drama Queen to Goddess Queen

Kelly Sullivan

Goddess Queen Unlimited
Topanga, California

Printed in Hong Kong

Kelly Sullivan's books and other products are available to order at:
www.goddessqueen.com
For copies of *Discover Your Inner Goddess Queen*
www.unlimitedpublishing.com/authors/1588320243.htm

Second Edition
ISBN: 0-9725582-1-7

Goddess Queen Unlimited
Topanga, California

Acknowledgements

I would like to extend oceans of gratitude to the following angels for helping me create this book:

- To Dana Walden, my love, soul mate, muse, for being the best partner, lover (not to mention editor), and for co-creating a life with me that is beyond my dreams!
- To Nirvana Gayle, for introducing me to my Goddess Queen.
- To Uncle Rich, for his inspiration, support, and "Up Your Attitude!"
- To Bruce McCullough, for his vision, support, and belief in me, and lending me the laptop that started all of this!
- To my Mom, for being my role model and a living example of unconditional love.
- To my Dad, for his amazing soul cooking and for letting me know how much he loves me.
- To Jeanene, for her oceanic generosity, support, and love.
- To Shannon, for teaching me about soulful authenticity.
- To Grandma Bishop, I know she's guiding me with her quiet strength.
- To Grandpa Bishop, for his sense of humor and playfulness.
- To Grandma "No Lace Curtains" Sullivan, thank you for being the matriarch that crochets the family together.
- To Jimmy and Cory Sullivan, for setting me up with my first PC!
- To J.W. Monkfish for teaching me to just be.
- To Reverend Michael, for being an example of "Spiritual Obedience."
- To Gypsy Racco, Bella and Luma for being cut from the same cloth as me, and our mystical friendship.
- To Nicole Venables, for being the greatest sponsor/angel…and for telling me I can have it all!

- To Firestar, for being a bright burst of divine light.
- To Jo-e Sutton, for extraordinary wisdom, love, council, and friendship.
- To Jody Sutton, my soul sister, for her integrity, Core Values, and for playing an integral part of the realization of the Goddess Queen Gathering.
- To Wendy Anton-Saez, for her effortless ease.
- To Malila Saez, for her big heart.
- To Helen Djukic, for her blazing spirit, and contagious enthusiasm.
- To Suzie Hirayabashi, for her "Open & Loving Heart."
- To Robert Silverstone, for teaching me to be "In the Moment."
- To Jovial Kemp, for teaching me "Awe-robics."
- To Carrabella Peart, for being an example of "Having it All!"
- To Stephen Powers, for demonstrating the true meaning of "Drive."
- To Shawndara Brady, for truly embodying friendship.
- To Nancy Allen, for our incarnations through life, from Brownies to Goddess.
- To D'ona Esparza, for permission to be creative, and to have fun.
- To Teresa Whitton, for being my blood-sister, tardy-twin, and so much more.
- To Celia Moore, for being a living angel whom I want to be like when I grow up.
- To Julia Cameron and Mark Bryon, for their masterpiece, "The Artist's Way."
- To Marianne Williamson, for being a mirror and role model.
- To all the benevolent beings both seen and unseen, thank you from the top to the bottom of my heart for your support, love, wisdom, guidance, encouragement, and belief in me and in this work! I love & appreciate you…

—Kelly

Table of Contents

Foreword / 1

   The Goddess Queen Connection / 2

   Questions / 6

   What Is a Goddess Queen? / 7

   Who Is This Journey For? / 8

   "The Face of a Goddess Queen" / 9

   Suggestions for a Successful Journey / 10

   My Journey / 10

   This World Needs Goddess Queens! / 15

   From Drama Queen to Goddess Queen... / 17

   Pillars of the Goddess Queen Temple / 19

   50 Pearls of Goddess Queen Wisdom / 19

   Goddess Queen Visioning / 23

   Goddess Queen Activations / 24

   Goddess Queen Rendezvous & Journaling / 25

   "If This Journal Could Talk" / 28

   The Drama Queen Rules of Survival / 29

   From Drama Queen to Goddess Queen / 30

   From Drama Queen to Goddess Queen Contract / 31

Week One: Meet Your Goddess Queen / 33

   Goddess Queen Prayer / 34

   "Stepping Out" / 35

   Four Questions to Help You Discover Your Goddess Queen / 36

   Pearls of Wisdom / 40

   Visioning / 41

   Activations / 43

Week Two: The Goddess Queen & Career / 43

Goddess Queen Divine Career Prayer / 46
"She Tries" / 47
Soul Blueprint / 48
Quotes for Contemplation / 49
The Goddess Queen Time Machine / 50
Pearls of Wisdom / 53
Visioning / 54
Activations / 56

Week Three: The Goddess Queen & Relationship / 59

The Goddess Queen Relationship Prayer / 60
"Twin Flame" / 61
Self-Love / 62
Tune Her In & Turn Her Up! / 64
"Wrapping Paper" / 66
Openhearted Discernment / 67
"Divine Relationship" / 70
Pearls of Wisdom / 72
Visioning / 73
Activations / 75

Week Four: The Goddess Queen & Creativity / 77

Goddess Queen Creativity Prayer / 78
"Sweetest Serenade" / 79
Wearing Your Soul on Your Sleeve / 81
"The Deep End of Your Ocean" / 83
Transform the Domain of Pain into the Space of Grace / 83
"The Dance of the Goddess Queen" / 86
Pearls of Wisdom / 87
Visioning / 88
Activations / 90

Week Five: The Goddess Queen & Abundance / 93

Goddess Queen Abundance Prayer / 94
"Butterfly Abundance" / 95
Out of the Lack Shack and into the Mansion of Expansion / 96
In Goddess We Trust / 97
Abundance Affirmation / 99
Transferring Commodities / 100
Pearls of Wisdom / 101
Visioning / 102
Activations / 104

Week Six: The Goddess Queen & Sex / 107

Sacred Sexuality Prayer / 108
"Ecstasy Dance" / 109
Make Love Not War / 110
"How Much Love Can I Handle?" / 112
Cleaning Your Goddess Queen Pool / 113
"Goddess Is My Name" / 115
The Goddess Queen 'IntimaC's / 116
Pearls of Wisdom / 118
Visioning / 119
Activations / 121

Week Seven: The Goddess Queen & Having It All / 125

Goddess Queen Having It All Prayer / 127
"I'm Free" / 128
The Circle of Elders / 129
Circle of Elders Meditation / 130
"On a Warm August Eve" / 131
Having It All / 132
Having It All Affirmations / 133
Heaven's Playground / 134
Pearls of Wisdom / 136
Pearl for the Rest of Your Life / 136
Visioning / 137
Activations / 139

Afterword / 141

Guidelines for a Goddess Queen Gathering / 143
Notes about Goddess Queen Gatherings / 145
Format for a Goddess Queen Gathering / 146

References / 150

Foreword

"When I first coined the phrase Goddess Queen it was to capture the essence of the divine feminine in both its heavenly and earthly state. The Goddess represented the feminine at the apex of its heavenly nature, and The Queen represented the epitome of the feminine in its earthly state. It was a way of honoring the highest feminine nature within every woman, and acknowledging that if they were not already there in consciousness, this was indeed their destiny.

However, at an even deeper level, the archetype of the Goddess throughout all of the traditions of the world is depicted in myriad form. There are images of the Goddess as warrior, nurturer, lover, creator, destroyer, wild, free, powerful, giving, playful, beautiful and the list goes on. To call forth the Goddess in a woman is to acknowledge the wonder, grace and beauty of that woman in what-ever form she is expressing, because in the traditions of the world, the Goddess has been so diverse in her expressions to be inclusive of every thing you can imagine. To call her a Queen on top of that is to acknowledge that she is standing in her spiritual authority and authenticity, boldly proclaiming, for all to see, her radiance, power and glory.

Kelly was one of the first women that I used this phrase in referencing her in a prayer. When she asked me if she could use the phrase Goddess-Queen as a series of workshops and then as the title in her book, I was honored, although to be quite frank, I never thought I had a corner on the market of that phrase in the first place. However, Kelly really embodies the grace and beauty, fire and passion, sensitivity and power of what the Goddess-Queen really represents. Her work with the sisterhood of chelas she has gathered around her has deeply enriched and illumined their lives. In this book, she shares some of that experience so that a larger audience of women can stand in the glory of their true Goddess-Queen nature, and men can stand up and honor them for who they really are.

As both women and men stand in bold testimony to the awesome power, beauty, grace and magnificence of the Goddess-Queen, we take our rightful place on the throne as Kings & Queens of the Most High. We embrace the Divine feminine and masculine within our own being and as whole-souled, fully mature spiritual beings, heal this sacred world we call Gaia, and reveal the kingdom of heaven here on earth."

Rev. Nirvana Reginald Gayle
Agape International Spiritual Center

The Goddess Queen Connection

I recall the very moment the concept of a "Higher Self" first dawned on me. It was the summer before 5th grade. I was sitting spellbound in the theatre, watching the movie "Grease." It was the scene in the Soda Shop, when *Frenchie,* (the *Pink Lady* with the neon hair) was expressing her big dilemma: "Should I drop out of High School, or go on to Beauty School?" She wished aloud for someone to give her advice and tell her what to do.

Then, lo and behold, in a burst of pink smoke, Frankie Avalon (her very own Goddess Queen...in drag) emerged out of the sky to tell her, "Go back to High School!" I realized then and there that when I am at a crossroads, all I need to do is sincerely ask for guidance, and be patient as the answers mysteriously (sometimes in the form of a musical comedy) reveal themselves to me. The source of Higher Wisdom is always here, waiting to bestow itself upon us...if we just ask!

In all tyrannical, or totalitarian governments/religions there has been one common denominator: the denial of the individual's own connection to their higher knowing. That way people are easily controlled and manipulated. It is my opinion that any course of study that doesn't ultimately refer a person back to his or her own inner guidance is ultimately doing the student a disservice. That way of teaching perpetuates a person's need to seek answers outside themselves. I can't count how many times I've left a seminar or finished reading a great book, and felt absolutely filled with the assurance that, "This time I've got it right". I would try implementing *their* techniques for the first few days, only to feel disillusioned. Even though the technique was brilliant, it didn't ever *address the real issue: that I was disconnected from my own inner wisdom and was grappling for a way to connect!* Like the saying goes, give a man a fish, you feed him for a day…teach a man to fish, you feed him for the rest of his life. Give a woman advice—you give her some temporary relief. Reintroduce her to her Goddess Queen, and you give her access to freedom, power and the confidence to last a lifetime…and then some!

In "The Pathwork of Transformation," Eva Pierrakos says, "As long as you cannot rely on your intuitive processes, you must be insecure and lacking in self-confidence. You try to make up for this by relying on others, or on false religion. This makes you weak and helpless. But if you have mature, strong emotions, you will trust yourself and therein find a security you never dreamed existed."

We begin the process of connecting with our inner Goddess Queen when we realize that we no longer have a choice, or when we see that doing things any other way is ridiculous and a complete waste of time. There are doors that we don't have to walk through any more. Not because we're holier than thou, but because we've literally *been there, done that, bought the tee shirt*—in fact, for some of us, a whole closet full of them! We are tired of the pain! Yes, we understand that pain is not completely avoidable in this life—but, with a direct and consistent connection to our inner Goddess Queen, the *unnecessary pain* in life is kept to a minimum. Like dross that becomes gold, this graceful Goddess Queen awareness turns ordinary pain into mystical pearls of wisdom through an alchemical dance of the soul!

Why is it so important to connect daily with your Highest Self? The answer is: because there is no such thing as a wasted day. Consider the crossroads we face daily: *Which way do I turn? Who am I? Who can I trust? Should I go back to school and get my degree? Where do I really want to live? Should I marry him? Should I have another child?* Then there are the mundane questions: *What should I wear on this interview? Should I exercise today? Should I eat the broccoli or one more piece of chocolate cake? Should I go out with that dangerously attractive man who's been calling?* If we seek it, we will find that there is no lack of external advice, or answers from other people to all our questions. What is unique about this Goddess Queen Paradigm is that it is not set up under the pretense that I, or anyone else for that matter, will be attempting to answer your questions for you, tell you what to do, fix you, change you, add anything to you, or even take anything away that seems to be hindering you. Because, honestly, *there is nothing about you that needs to be fixed! You already are perfect, whole, and complete right here and now; all the answers you've ever wanted to know are already within you—and have been since before the beginning of time!* Your inner Goddess Queen cannot be manipulated, outsmarted, dumbfounded, or confused in any way. The Goddess Queen is the part of you that is *consistent*—she won't let you down. This Mystical Inner Being has all the answers to any questions that arise in life. As role models, wives, girlfriends, mothers, matriarchs, friends, politicians, daycare workers, we *must* be connected with the part of us that is the highest. We then can go to sleep at night with a smile on our face and wake up in the morning with a spring in our step because we know that we are *fulfilling our intention for incarnating in this dimension!*

I also advocate what in Buddhism is called "Beginner's Mind." Beginner's Mind states that you must be empty of your own self-knowledge, in order to receive anything new. At first glance, Beginner's Mind might seem to invalidate this Goddess Queen Paradigm. The truth is, it doesn't. However, there is a delicate balance, a razor's edge, between these two wisdom paths. They do not contradict each other so much as they run parallel to one another. Your charge is to discern between what is appropriate at any given moment; when to be as a baby, open and receptive, and when to sit on your throne and claim your authority as a Goddess Queen; when to release your small reference points (i.e. the limited, fear-based thinking that keeps you stuck in unworkable habits and patterns), and when to remain steadfast, connected, and immersed in the reference point of your Goddess Queen.

Always remember that within you is a divine spark of infinite intelligence that exists above the clouds of your human, limited, linear thinking. When you align yourself with your inherent connection to this divine spark from the Absolute Source of all Love and Intelligence, you embody a natural confidence and authority that will up-level the quality of your life, and the lives of those around you!

"Heaven is already perfect. It's Earth we must improve. The key to doing this is to keep our minds on the thoughts of Heaven, while grounding our bodies to Earth. The reunification of these two realms is the goal of human evolution." (Smith)

"What? You say. 'Me, a goddess?' Yes, I say, and don't act so surprised. You knew when you were little that you were born for something special and no matter what happened to you, that couldn't be erased. The magic couldn't be drained from your heart any more than Lady MacBeth could wash the guilt from her hands. Sorry to tell you, but you had it right years ago and then you forgot. You were born with a mystical purpose. In reading this now you might remember what it is." (Williamson)

Questions

Before you continue, answer the following questions:

What would it be like if you could count on your inner guidance?

What would you do if you knew that the place inside you that held the answers to life's questions was consistent and reliably accessible?

If your Higher Awareness was running your life, what might change or be different?

What would you have to give up in order to embrace the fact that your Inner Wise Woman is alive within you now?

How would embracing your inner wise Woman affect your Career? Relationships? Health? Finances? Creativity? Self-expression? Sex life?

To find out about who your inner Goddess Queen is, and how to connect with her, read on...

"If a glimpse in the media of a female role model can have such important impact on the lives of women, how much more profound might be the activating and calling forth of an archetype within her?" (Steinem)

Webster's Dictionary Defines:

Goddess: A female God; A woman whose charm or beauty arouses adoration.

Queen: A female monarch notable for rank, power, or attractiveness.

What Is a Goddess Queen?

From an archetypal perspective, the Goddess represents a loving, heavenly being of wisdom and light. The Queen represents one who has earthly stature, commands respect, authority, love, and power. From my perspective, one without the other is incomplete. In this day and age, the Goddess without the Queen, might be wondrously spiritual and delicious, but, perhaps, in need of some solidity and a degree of worldly savvy. The Queen, though mighty and glorious, might leave a bit to be desired if all of her energy were narrow-mindedly focused on this tangible, material, linear, three-dimensional world.

But, put them both together, and what do you have? A Heavenly, wise, loving woman that embodies Eternal Truths and mysteries, combined with a solid, regal, royal and grounded human woman. It is in identifying with the combination of these significant archetypes that empowers women to anchor Heaven on Earth!

"Freedom consists not in refusing to recognize anything above us, but in respecting something which is above us: for by respecting it we raise ourselves to it, and by our very acknowledgment, prove that we bear within ourselves what is higher, and are worthy to be on a level with it." (Goethe)

"The Soul intuitively seeks the perfect circumstance and situation now needed to heal wrong thoughts and bring you the rightful experience of Who You Really Are. It is the Soul's intention to know itself experientially—and thus to know me. For the Soul understands that you and I are one, even as the mind denies this truth and the body acts out this denial. Therefore, *in moments of great decision, be out of your mind, and do some Soul searching instead. The Soul understands what the mind cannot conceive.*" (Walsh)

Who Is This Journey For?

A participant in one of my Goddess Queen Gatherings once shamefully admitted to me, "I don't feel like I should come to the Gathering tonight because I'm really going through a difficult time in my life right now and I'm not feeling very Goddess Queen-*esque.*"

I responded to her in the same way I always respond to a statement like this, "First of all, the Goddess Queen in you doesn't *need* to read this book, listen to the CD's, do the exercises, or attend this workshop. That would be like taking a fish to swimming lessons! The Goddess Queen already knows how to be a Goddess Queen! This book is specifically designed for the part of you that doesn't have a clue about who the Goddess Queen is. When you are challenged by some 'life' circumstance, that is the *best* time to come to the group."

Whether you are just beginning or are well on your way, the Goddess Queen Path will support and uplift you.

The Face of a Goddess Queen

Dare to vision,
Dare to believe,
Your heart's deepest desires,
In a mystical reprieve.
Surrender to your depths,
Surrender to your heights,
Embrace all of your shadows,
With your rainbow colored lights.
Dive deep into your mysteries,
Your uncharted terrain,
Let your tidal wave swallow you whole,
And bring you back from whence you came.
On your magic carpet you'll fly,
High above the land,
Illumining the path for your insatiable Soul,
That hungers to understand.
The thunder of the silence,
The splendor of True Grace,
And when you've made your way home
To Heaven within,
You'll see your Goddess Queen's face.

Suggestions for a Successful Journey

1. Use the spaces provided in this workbook to write down your visions and inspirations.

2. Do the weekly Visioning, Rendezvous, Activations, and Journaling as they are outlined in the book.

3. Participate solo or create your own weekly "Goddess Queen Gathering."

4. Listen to the CDs that will guide you through the Prayers, Meditations, Visionings, and Activations.

5. Follow The 50 Pearls Of Goddess Queen Wisdom for the next seven weeks.

6. Enjoy yourself and have a magnificent journey!

My Journey

One day, as I was in the agony of the break-up with my ex-boyfriend, confusion settled upon me like a dark, thick blanket of L.A. smog. My heart was split in two. I struggled with why I stepped out of what seemed like the 'perfect' relationship. This was a man who was wonderful. He treated me like a queen. He met every qualification on my list. I judged myself harshly because I thought I was sabotaging the one chance I had to actually be in a loving, healthy relationship. But I could no longer deny the fact that in order to see him, I had to fight to peel myself away from whatever it was I was doing...painting my toenails...scrubbing the dishes, etc. It was as if he was a plate of spinach, and I was a stubborn, pouting child, with my inner mother coercing me, "Eat this…it's good for you…trust me…it'll make you strong…you'll thank me when you're older!"

I reflected upon the nickname that was given to me during a weekend relationship course I had just attended: "Black Widow" was the name…one who lures men into a fatal web of love, and leaves them wounded and lifeless. "That's what you are, Kelly; that's all you'll ever be" I abusively chastised myself, "After all these years of supposed 'spiritual growth', here you are again, doing the same ol' thing you've always done. How many more guys are you going to do this to? Huh? Who are you kidding, you'll never change," etc.

The enormous guilt I felt pushed me over the edge into a Pandora's box of deep despair. Talk about a dark night of the soul! So, I did all I know how to do in a situation like that. I cried, and I cried, and when I was done, I cried some more. When I was done with that, and I felt I had no more tears left, I found myself curled up in a very humble prayer (a good idea at a time like this). I prayed to see my situation the way God saw it. I prayed to see the unconscious habits and patterns that were in my blind spot. I prayed for clarity so that I might be able to do something different next time ("If there is a next time," I thought cynically).

There I sat, on my bed, in absolute silence (except for the occasional sniffle from my chaffed, red nose), waiting for Divine guidance…for God to speak to me, a bush to burn…*anything!* There was nothing but the hum of the silence. I found myself staring blankly at my bedroom wall, waiting, waiting, waiting…And then it began. The projector in my mind began to play the movie of my entire romantic history. Over and over, all the similarities, all the common denominators from all my past "failed" attempts at love. It was all very dramatic ("Excellent soap opera material," I appraised).

"Look, I don't mean to sound ungrateful," I said to God, "I really do appreciate you going to all this trouble to reveal what has been lurking in my blind spot. However, I think I've got the picture. You really don't have to keep playing this horror movie again and again. The least you could do is stick a happy ending to this tragedy and give me some sort of clue how to undo this pattern! How about it? Is that too much to ask?

I'll do anything you want. I promise I'll learn my lesson this time. Please show me what to do. Please show me a way out!"

Nothing came to me immediately, except the certainty that I could *not* do this dance anymore. That was painfully clear! And what, pray tell, was "this dance?" All I could surmise was that as far back as I could remember I was drawn to men that seemed to really know who they were. For the most part, I would agree with their basic philosophy, and jump on their bandwagon. Since they were so certain that their perspective was the right one, how could I go wrong? What would happen was that they would fall "in love" with me (of course they would, who wouldn't fall in love with someone who completely fit the mold of their perfect partner...someone who was willing to live completely on their terms?). As soon as they would fall "in love" with me, I would be shocked into the realization that it was not me they were in love with, but the possibility that I represented as their ideal mate. I was frantically trying to be their "dream girl" not because I was intentionally trying to trick them, but because I didn't have a core sense of my authentic self. Or if I did, I did not trust it, or believe that it was loveable enough to keep a man interested. Knowing that it was just a matter of time before I would fall off my fantasy pedestal, and angry that they couldn't see through my smokescreen, I would have to leave. The man would be devastated and I would feel shell-shocked and guilt-ridden.

In this moment of illumination, I quickly phoned my Practitioner (spiritual counselor, "Nirvana"- appropriately named) and scheduled a session. When I shakingly came to see him, I felt like a tattered and weather-beaten alley cat.

After a few moments of quieting me down, and despite my resistance, he led me on a guided excursion into a sacred place, a majestic chamber where I came face to face with a very wise, loving, and powerful being. She was radiantly beautiful, so bright I had to squint. She was standing tall and proud, with soft, loving, compassionate eyes, bursting with the glow of royal self-esteem. There was not an ounce of her that was hurting, aching, struggling, wanting for anything—or anyone. She was the Divine Incarnate. Her arms spread wide to reveal her jeweled robe that had been woven out of light and magic. She was completely connected to the source of all Creation. As she invited me to come near, I humbly obliged ...who was I to say no? As I moved closer, I discovered that she wasn't such a foreign being after all. I saw that her face was actually my face, her smile...my smile, her heart...my heart...her energy...my energy. This awesome, loving Queen was in fact...me...at my fullest potential...my Highest Self! I bowed at her feet and she extended her arms inviting me in. I gratefully accepted, and allowed my hurt and pain to be melted by her embrace. As I sobbed in her arms like a frightened child reuniting with its mother...my burdens dissolved.

When my tears subsided, I felt clean and clear for the first time in a long, long, long time...She whispered in my ear, with a voice that sounded like an angelic choir, "I am your Goddess Queen—the part of you that has been around since before the Beginning of Time. I am all knowing, all seeing, and all wise. I am the one within you that holds all the answers to every question you've ever sought. My heart is large enough to contain all of you...all of your pain, fear, doubt, worry, insecurity and shame. I have enough love for the entire world...and beyond! And if you allow me to, I will gladly and joyously guide your life, whenever, wherever you want, need, or desire...unconditionally."

In that one session, my entire life changed. I discovered that although I appreciated all of the self-improvement courses, seminars, and workshops I've attended, (and, indeed there have been many) *all the answers I have ever sought were right inside of me!* Yes, I know, the phrase, "All of the answers are within me" gets thrown around in spiritual circles, like a Frisbee. But, on that day, I grasped the true meaning of the phrase. That simple guided meditation literally changed the way I now see *everything!* Since that moment, everything in my life has been turned upside down. Believe me, it needed to be...my relationships, the way I feel, think, and go about my career...absolutely every aspect of my life! I must say, the way in which I've been most affected, is that I seldom ever feel confused...and when I do, it's simply a matter of moments before I connect with my inner Goddess Queen. Then all that needs to be revealed in that moment is revealed, and I am at peace. Interestingly, connecting with my inner Goddess Queen is not always a tremendously enchanting, mystical experience. Sometimes it's quite mundane. I don't always have to do a formal "eyes closed, sage, candle and incense burning meditation" to connect with her. I can be driving through traffic and just simply ask the question, "What would my Goddess Queen do right now?" and instantly a higher perspective is revealed to me.

No More Band-Aids

The following day, after this initial visioning, I found myself unable to speak...all I could do was write, I didn't even stop to eat. Thoughts came pouring through me at lightning speed. As I was writing, I reflected upon the many conversations I've had with friends, clients, and siblings, about the challenges and solutions life presents to us each day. I thought about how ravenous we have all been to find answers to life's most provocative questions. I thought about the mountains of books, strategies, techniques, band-aids, and magic potions we've shared. I realized that, like a drug, all of these "answers" would only numb our pain temporarily until the next breakdown. Then we'd grab for another "band-aid" that would give us a false sense of, "ahhhh, I've finally got it right this time" and the drama cycle would continue...leaving us more desperate and cynical than ever before.

What felt so overwhelmingly profound about this concept of connecting with my own inner Goddess Queen, is that it goes far beyond technique, it goes far beyond a "quick fix"...it goes far beyond a hip trend or band-aid...and it even goes far beyond the confines of this book! This book, this concept, is a springboard, a catalyst for something so much greater than anything that could be put into print. It goes far beyond the pompousness and arrogance of the intellect. This book is intended to create a reunion between you and your Highest Self...the source of your own wisdom...between you and your Goddess Queen!

A Historical Look at the Goddess Queen

Now that I understand Goddess Queen Consciousness, I can step back from my individual life and look at this as a societal rite of passage as well.

During the early 1940s, there was World War II and all relationships, careers, and creative energies were focused on survival. Toward the end of the 40's and into the 50's a collective sigh of relief was heard around the country because we were finally at peace. Energy could now be spent on *living* instead of just merely *existing*. But, the trend was extremely conservative as we were transitioning out of the shock of war. There wasn't a lot of encouragement for women to express themselves…in fact, just the opposite. It was just a matter of time before women (and all of society for that matter) exploded. And that explosion marked the entrance of the 1960s—where sex, drugs, and Grace Slick were the order of the day. Women were on the hunt for their true authentic place in the world. This Evolution Revolution continued into the 1970s with even more drugs, promiscuity, and searching. The pendulum began to swing toward a more conservative direction in the 80's with the AIDS epidemic. People were tending toward a more prudent way of life. In the 90's, women were becoming more introspectively spiritual with gurus, teachers, spirit guides, psychics, crystals, and Shamans, guiding their way.

Now in this new millennium, the time for searching is over. The message is no longer to wait for a Messiah to magically appear at your doorstep…or to wait for the answers to come from anyone, anywhere, or anything outside of yourself. The time has come to now *be the answer!*

This World Needs Goddess Queens!

I was coming out of Ralph's grocery store and I noticed a woman with a child. I'll call her *Marge*. She was trying to back her car out of a parking space while being scowled at by another woman. I'll call her *Betty*. Betty was also trying to back out of a parking space. Apparently, Marge was in such a hurry to get to where she was going that she left her shopping cart behind Betty's car. Betty was also frantically trying to get to where she was going. They exchanged exasperated looks at each other as Marge screeched away in a huff. Enraged, Betty hastily jerked the shopping cart out of her way, cursing under her breath. She slammed the door of her car, seething, as she skidded out of the parking lot.

Who knows where they were going—but the lucky person awaiting them was sure to get the backlash of this interaction. As I've sometimes joked, "The only thing scarier than a reactive man ...is a reactive woman!"

Whose fault was this? Who cares? Either we are being our Goddess Queen, or we aren't! And when we aren't, we can be *sooo scary!* Nurse Ratchet, Cruella Deville, eat your hearts out.

The question is: How deeply do our actions and attitudes affect each other?

The answer is: More profoundly than we can fathom.

Had Marge been connected with her inner Goddess Queen, she probably wouldn't have left her basket behind Betty's car in the first place. And if she had left it there, she would have apologized, smiled warmly, and moved her basket. This would have been a reminder for Betty to catch her breath, unclench her fists, show a bit of compassion, and bring her Goddess Queen to her next appointment. This, in turn, would remind whomever she would be interacting with to do the same, and so on, and so on, causing a ripple effect of kindness and compassion. One negative, unconscious act provokes another... just as one Goddess Queen act inspires another!

Can we really afford to go one more precious day without tapping into our Goddess Queen power? Everywhere we look is a call for more Goddess Queens: politics, the inner city, relationships, the economy, child rearing, etc. As a very wise friend of mine used to say, "You're either on the side of the problem, or on the side of the solution!" Which side are you on? Imagine...if just for one day, we were all in our Goddess Queen Power ...not just women, but men also in their Divine King Power—what would happen? What would there be to report on the news? What would the city streets look like? What would happen to the economy…our collective blood pressure…the world political crisis? It would be astounding! We might not know what to do with ourselves! It would be beautiful!

From Drama Queen to Goddess Queen…
In Three Acts

It's time for us to grow up and stop being narcissistic, nit-picky, spoiled, self-centered, egotistical, spongy, greedy, sniveling, little brats, whining about the fact that "our concept" of the world has let us down. *It was supposed to! That's its job! Don't ya get it?*

Act I of this story called "Your Life" begins with you as a fresh, innocent perfect, precious, naïve, gullible little child. You are pure, authentic, radiant, and beautiful.

Act II begins when you are either betrayed, tricked, manipulated, devastated, or somehow cast out of your innocence. Something happens, or many things happen that cause you to feel the world is no longer a safe place. As your identity comes crashing down, you adopt a mask …a new way of being that covers up your authentic self—as well as a *Drama Queen Modus Operandi* (DQMO) to help you survive in this very hostile world. This is a wonderful plan until your DQMO begins to have diminishing returns, and your inauthentic self begins to get you into more trouble than you could ever imagine. Act II ends with you on your knees, pleading to God…to the universe…to anybody for help.

Act III begins in a state of grace. You are extremely humble because the identity that you've attached yourself to is no longer running the show. Although you are disoriented and puzzled, you are simultaneously relieved, and extremely grateful that God/Goddess is now informing your life. Once you regain your balance, you realize that what didn't kill you makes you stronger…and because you are an eternal being, *even that which kills you makes you stronger!* You realize that this world is much larger, and you are much greater than you ever perceived…you transcend the former identity and begin to finally get on with the business of living a powerful, purposeful authentic life…far beyond the meager existence you were willing to settle for. As you travel deeper into this awareness, you become a Wayshower for others, holding the light and opening doors for many people. Your life begins to be inspired and motivated by a higher purpose, and you begin to help others who are still gasping for air. You remind them that Act II is over—it's intermission—time to get ready for Act III! Act III is where the magic happens—where the Damsel in Distress regains her power, and is transformed into a Mystical Queen.

This is good news! Access into your Divine Goddess Queen Self actually requires that you not even lift a finger. Goddessness, (Do you like how I create my own words?) is as effortless as slipping into a nice, warm, bubble bath. To be a Goddess Queen, *let go* of all the identities you've been straining to maintain, and return to your essential nature. As they say, "It only requires faith the size of a mustard seed to move a mountain!" It's really simple…but, sometimes, it may not be easy (depending upon the attachment you have to your Drama Queen habits and identity.) Learning to trust that the Goddess Queen within you knows what she's doing means that we can stop resisting at any time we like. This is the key to unraveling her mystery. If you just have that tiny ounce of willingness, and demonstrate that willingness by taking the action that it inspires, then before you know it, you will look in the mirror and your Goddess Queen will be the one looking back at you!

Her time has come! She's like a magical genie that's been "bottled" up inside for eons.

Uncork her before she pops! If not for you, then for your family, your friends, co-workers, homeless people on the street, hungry children in Africa, your next-door neighbor or the checkout clerk at Ralph's, for Goddess' sake!

There are hearts that are breaking at this very moment, lives that are falling apart, nervous breakdowns, suicide, loneliness, despair, and heartache in epidemic proportions…Enough whining, you've played your part in Act II (a Tony award is sure to come). Intermission is over, the house lights are dimming, the curtain is rising, and the orchestra is swelling. Get ready, get set (drum roll, please). Here she comes, the one we've all been waiting for; the one we've traveled all this way to see; the one, the only...The Goddess Queen!

Pillars of the Goddess Queen Temple

The following are the foundational anchoring tools that will help you to construct and upkeep your Goddess Queen Temple:

50 Pearls of Goddess Queen Wisdom
Visioning
Activations
Goddess Queen Rendezvous
Journaling: Dreams, Gratitude List, Uncensored Downloading

50 Pearls of Goddess Queen Wisdom

The following exercise is suggested as an enhancement to your Goddess Queen experience. If you would like to, go to a bead or fabric store and buy fifty beads or pearls and a long necklace string. Place the "pearls" in a pouch or bag. Each morning of your journey, take a pearl from your pouch and read the Goddess Queen pearl for the day. For example, if today is your first day of your journey, then you would read pearl #1. Pay close attention to what it evokes in you and take note of your insights. Carry your pearl around with you each day, either in your purse or pocket to be a tactile reminder of the specific aspect of Goddess Queen Consciousness that you are embodying (don't leave home without it!) The following morning, place the pearl from the previous day on the string, pick out a new pearl and begin again. By the time you've completed this seven-week journey, you will have created your very own Goddess Queen Pearls of Wisdom Necklace; akin to Tibetan Prayer beads or Catholic Rosary beads, the Goddess Queen Pearls of Wisdom will become a grounding tool to assist you in anchoring Goddess Queen Consciousness into your daily life.

Pearls for Week One:

Day #1: Live today as if it were your last.

Day #2: Cultivate a hunger for transformation.

Day #3: Act as if all of your heart's desires were already fulfilled.

Day #4: Focus more on who you are becoming and less on who you used to be.

Day #5: At every crossroads consult the wisdom of your Goddess Queen.

Day #6: Make your decisions from the place in you that knows you are whole, perfect and complete.

Day #7: Every time you see your reflection in anything, look into your eyes and say, "You are the most gorgeous and amazing Goddess Queen I've ever seen!"

Pearls for Week Two:

Day #8: Honor all of your feelings (all of them) as sacred.

Day #9: Make enough room inside your heart for all aspects of your personality.

Day #10: Imagine your Goddess Queen is beside you all day today. Don't leave home without her!

Day #11: Treat yourself as if you were your own child. Be kind to yourself today when you stumble or fall.

Day #12: Know that when your buttons get pressed you are at your edge, on the verge of breaking into a greater, more authentic expression of yourself.

Day #13: If you are going through a crisis, or a difficult time, remember to keep your attention on the feeling tone of this new, beautiful self that is birthing.

Day #14: Stand up for yourself if someone's hurtful or inappropriate to you.

Pearls for Week Three:

Day #15: Behave as if you were the most loved being on the planet.

Day #16: Know that whether or not they show it, everyone you see loves you.

Day #17: Become a magnet for synchronicities by looking for them and acknowledging them.

Day #18: When in doubt, open your heart and love.

Day #19: Imagine that you have special powers that allow you to see through people's hurts, illusions, and aberrant behavior, into the depths of their radiant magnificence.

Day #20: Be Present. It is the greatest gift you can give yourself or someone you love.

Day #21: Treat every person you see, especially those who challenge you, as if they were your own precious children.

Pearls for Week Four:

Day #22: Give your inner child permission to run the show today (let her dress you up, take you out!)

Day #23: Intentionally take a detour down a road you've never been down before.

Day #24: Imagine how you would feel if your greatest challenge or conflict was resolved. Carry this feeling with you throughout your day.

Day #25: Go to a fabric store and get a swatch of colorful fabric that inspires you. Carry it around with you today.

Day #26: Love and appreciate yourself for being absolutely magnificent just as you are.

Day #27: Treat each challenge as if it were a BID (a Blessing In Disguise).

Day #28: In the midst of any storm, dive into the center where your creativity and power lives.

Pearls for Week Five:

Day #29: Explore how you can widen your capacity to love
and to be loved.

Day #30: Pay all debts, or at least make arrangements to clear
them.

Day #31: Spend today feeling as though you were the
wealthiest woman on the planet.

Day #32: As you raise your consciousness, give yourself a raise
(up your salary!)

Day #33: Be generous with "I love you's" and mean it!

Day #34: Live from the overflow: Give away ten items that you
no longer hold as precious.

Day #35: Imagine that each person you come across today is a
King or a Queen in disguise.

Pearls for Week Six:

Day #36: Say, "Yes!" to adventure, opportunities, and
invitations!

Day #37: Add something sexy or Goddess-like to your
wardrobe.

Day #38: Wear your favorite perfume for no particular reason.

Day #39: Wear a scarf or some flowing fabric and dance around
your house to your favorite music.

Day #40: Dip into sensuality with a Goddess Queen bath. Add
candles, incense, soft music, and privacy.

Day #41: Live today from your "G-spot" (Goddess spot)...as
if you knew that you were the most desirable woman in
the world.

Day #42: Write yourself a love letter and praise yourself lavishly
for being Goddess' gift to this world!

Pearls for Week Seven:

Day #43: Tie up all loose ends (i.e. if applicable, make apologies, or arrangements to pay off any debts, or complete unfinished business).

Day #44: Give yourself permission to make mistakes today and record them in your journal.

Day #45: Apply the wisdom you learned from your "mistakes" yesterday.

Day #46: Allow, "I can have it all" to be your mantra today.

Day #47: Extend your love and service to another person today as a demonstration of the loving and generous Goddess Queen that you are.

Day #48: Make a Self-appreciation list of all the things you've discovered about yourself over the past seven weeks.

Day #49: Acknowledge three people today for the positive contribution they've made to your life over these seven weeks.

Pearl for the Rest of Your Life:

Day #50: Let your light shine. Remember that the more you radiate, the brighter your world becomes!

Goddess Queen Visioning

Visioning is a tool that will assist you in creating an out-picturing of your Soul's blueprint. By consciously releasing your pre-conceived ideas and dwelling inside certain evocative questions, you make yourself available to gain a glimpse of your highest possibilities—your inner Goddess Queen! Many life changes have been inspired by Visioning. In fact this book is a product of visioning.

Remember, that the highest reality of your Goddess Queen is already a reality in Divine Mind. As the full potential of the mighty oak tree is active and alive in miniature within the acorn, so is your highest potential alive within you now. It is simply by asking the questions and remaining receptive and open, that your Goddess Queen is realized in your life. It is in consciously accessing your highest self that your own specific "Enlightenment Process" is quickened. What previously seemed to be insurmountable challenges in your life, will suddenly become manageable. Your highest dreams and aspirations will be achieved with velocity and ecstasy! In order to make the most of this experience and gain maximum results, I suggest that you create a ceremonial atmosphere for yourself. To prepare for a profound journey into the deepest regions of your being:

- Close the door to the outside world
- Light some candles and incense
- Turn off all phones and pagers
- Recline in a comfortable chair or bubble bath
- Keep your Goddess Queen Journal and a pen nearby to write down your visions, insights, and inspirations
- Turn on your "Goddess Queen Visioning" CD and/or read the Visioning Questions to yourself
- Allow the Queendom of Heaven to be revealed!

Goddess Queen Activations

On the last page of each chapter you will find Goddess Queen Activations. These are a blend of *Activities* and *Incantations* that will bring your Goddess Queen Visions into *Manifestation*. The Goddess Queen Activations are grounding tools, different ways for you to physicalize the Goddess Queen that you are coming to realize! Read the Activations at the beginning of each week, so that you will have plenty of time to do them throughout the week.

Goddess Queen Rendezvous & Journaling

A Goddess Queen Rendezvous is a 15-60 minute block of time that you spend getting acquainted with your Goddess Queen. Pick an outer or inner excursion that is fun and uplifting (i.e. going to an art exhibit, window shopping, sampling expensive perfumes in a pricey boutique, taking yourself to tea, getting a massage, facial, or pedicure, turning up the music when there's no one home and dancing like a wild woman). Your Goddess Queen Rendezvous is an exclusive date for you and your Goddess Queen. It doesn't have to cost you a penny; but the riches gained will be innumerable!

There are three aspects to the Goddess Queen Journaling: *Dreams, Gratitude Lists* and *Uncensored Downloading*. These two to three pages are to be written every day during the course of this workshop. Write them, ideally, first thing in the morning.

Dreams

As soon as you wake up in the morning, write in your Goddess Queen Journal whatever you can remember from your nighttime dreams. By acknowledging your dreams (the profound ones, the nightmares, and even the seemingly trivial ones), you are fortifying the bridge between your Conscious and Sub-Conscious Mind, deeply enhancing your conscious awareness of your deeper wisdom, intuition, and knowing. Don't be surprised if your dreams start to become very vivid. You are setting off on a very intense transformational process, you can add velocity to this journey by acknowledging what your Sub-Conscious mind is attempting to release and embody. If you become aware that you are having many nightmares during this process, do not be alarmed. This is actually a good sign. This simply means that your Sub-Conscious Mind is weeding out old thought forms that no longer serve you, and making room for new, more empowering ones to take root. In other words: *out with the old, and in with the new!*

Gratitude List

Write a list of ten things that you are grateful for each day, for example: your health, a good night's sleep, good friends, family, the new bathroom rug, the fact that you are on this magnificent journey, etc. A thankful attitude is inherent in Goddess Queen Consciousness. As you become proficient in the art of Gratitude, you will notice yourself becoming grateful even for the areas of life that challenge you. In hindsight we see that our deepest challenges often reward us with our greatest gifts. You will find that from the mountain top perspective, everything in life from the seeming good to the seeming bad is all worthy of our gratitude. It is all serving to deepen our capacity for love, wisdom, and compassion!

Uncensored Downloading

I feel that Uncensored Downloading is actually an act of "Soul-Mending." The pen represents the needle, and the words that pour through me onto the page are the thread, the paper represents my soul that is being stitched up with every word. When I sit down to write, sometimes I can feel so frazzled, but, within a few moments of uncensored downloading, I feel peace wash over me, the fog begins to lift, solutions and 'Aha's begin to surface.

Fill two pages with stream-of-consciousness writing in your Goddess Queen Journal. Ask questions regarding anything that may be currently troubling or concerning you, and see what shows up. Or use these two pages to vent. Sometimes venting is necessary in order to get to the gold under the surface. Do make sure to honor yourself by keeping your journal in a sacred and secret place so that no one will be tempted to invade your privacy. Doing this will give you the freedom to write without censoring, without trying to sound interesting, intelligent, poetic, brilliant, or profound. Give yourself full permission to write anything and everything that your mind, heart, or soul needs to release.

This book is a product of Visioning and Uncensored Downloading! You never know, sometimes in the midst of some serious spewing, some of the most profound and life changing insights are revealed. Actually, I will go so far as to say, (and I must thank Julia Cameron and Mark Bryan for creating the very inspirational book, "The Artist's Way), that writing in this way, has altered the entire trajectory of my life. I am convinced that by doing this three step process of daily journaling (dreams, gratitude list, and uncensored downloading), you will find your way back to your true, authentic, Goddess Queen Power.

Please give yourself the gift of this tool. If it is uncomfortable and you think there's nothing to write about, then write about your discomfort. Remember, even on the most neutral, bland, and colorless days, there are rubies and diamonds to uncover!

If This Journal Could Talk

If this journal could talk,
I bet I know what it would say:
"How mysterious the events are
That unfold for me each day!"
I never have a clue
About what each new page will behold,
Or what roller-coaster adventure
Is about to unfold.
This book is sacred;
It's the story of my life;
Puzzle pieces of my heart and soul;
All the joys and strife.
In these torn and tattered pages,
With coffee stains inside;
Is where all the complex mysteries
Of my spirit reside.
Sometimes it's poetry;
Sometimes it's spew.
But, it's my therapist, lover,
Best-friend true blue.
I thank God
For this very simple little book,
A place to vent my feelings;
So years later, I may look…
Back to see my growth,
All the lessons WELL learned,
The tears, the sorrow,
And all the corners I've turned.
This is my testament
To this life that I've been given,
To be left to my children's children,
Once I return to heaven.

The Drama Queen Rules of Survival

The following is from a work in progress that I am writing with Ruth de Sosa and Firestar, entitled, "Goddess In A Pinch…How To Be Heavenly When All Hell Is Breaking Loose."

On this Inspirational Journey from Drama Queen to Goddess Queen, it is important to clearly identify both aspects of yourself. By now I'm sure you are acquainted with, at least in theory, your inner Goddess Queen. And I'm sure that you are already aware of your inner Drama Queen. But, just in case there are any doubts, the following Drama Queen Rules Of Survival will paint the picture quite clearly.

1. Blame everyone for your problems.
2. Complain about everything.
3. Gossip as often as possible.
4. Look for the negative in all situations.
5. Should anything good ever happen, make sure to remind yourself it won't last. The other shoe is about to drop.
6. Keep in mind that there is no higher power at work, and you are absolutely alone in this big, scary world.
7. Whether asked or not, be ready to tell the sob story of your life at a moments notice.
8. No matter how much someone says they love you, they really don't. They are just saying it to get something from you.
9. Keep yourself up late at night inventing new ways to catastrophize the coming day.
10. Create as many psychosomatic illnesses as you possibly can.
11. When anyone apologizes to you, give them a cold unforgiving stare.
12. Be as rigid and inflexible as possible.
13. Expect perfection from everyone; and when they let you down, become devastated and furious.

14. Cultivate the ability to become hysterical over insignificant daily events.
15. Spread bad news quickly.
16. Turn everything, no matter how trivial, into a drama.
17. In every situation, project the absolute worst-case scenario.

Keep in mind that this description of the Drama Queen is not to be used to beat ourselves up. When we catch ourselves being identified with the Drama Queen, we are simply to become aware. Once we are aware, we then have the power to choose who we want to be, and what energy we prefer to orchestrate our lives!

From Drama Queen to Goddess Queen

Carefully consider the following agreement before committing to it. After all, signing and dating this document may have life altering implications. Be sure to realize that this is not about "getting rid of" your inner Drama Queen. We all know by now that there is no getting rid of her. She is part of the package and she is coming along for the ride, like it or not. If we try to bind, gag, and shove her in the trunk of our Goddess-Mobile, surely she will pry her way out. When she does, there will be hell to pay.

This is an agreement to reassign your Drama Queen to the role of "Passenger" and your Goddess Queen to the role of "Driver." If you do this, you will be surprised at how beautiful the journey will become. Most potholes will be avoided, but there will be an occasional detour or flat tire along the road toward Goddess Mountain. As the challenges are met without resistance and drama, your energy will be boosted, and lessons will be learned. And regardless of the bumps, you will realize that The Goddess Queen Highway is always paved in gold.

From Drama Queen to Goddess Queen Contract

I, _____, do hereby declare, on this _____ of _____, on behalf of myself, The Great Goddess Queen, and all living beings, to draw a line in the sand in which I leave behind my attachment, obsession, and investment in having my inner Drama Queen running the affairs of my life. With every breath, I receive the gifts of fresh inspiration, enthusiasm, and a sense of renewed vitality and freedom. I align to that which is highest, most truthful, and loving within me.

I, _____, do hereby reclaim my Heart from the bondage of fear, my Spirit from the chains of criticism, and my wings from the shackles of limitation.

I, _____, do hereby renounce self-pity, righteous resentments, perfectionism, victim-hood, and tantrums from running my life any longer.

Furthermore, I, _____, do hereby renounce the right of my Drama Queen, to make my decisions, choose my relationships, enter into commitments, or to affect my life's direction.

Finally, I, _____, from this day forward, now step across this threshold and integrate, marinate, and saturate my inner Drama Queen with the wisdom of my inner Goddess Queen; marrying my Humanity with my Divinity; thus bridging Heaven and Earth. This merging now expands my inner radiance, joy, healing power, wisdom, and self-love exponentially with every step I take. I now exhale a sigh of relief knowing that my burdens have been lifted, and my Goddess wings are now back in place. The time has come for me to soar to the top of Goddess Mountain and reclaim my rightful stature as a being of pure love, a Goddess Queen. I give thanks for this declaration, knowing that it is true, and so it is, now and forever.

Signature: _____ Date: _____

Post this near your prayer altar, on your bathroom mirror, refrigerator, or keep it in your purse. Renew your vows daily. Remember, you have not banished your Drama Queen, but you have simply changed her title to "Passenger." You have allowed your Higher Self to take the wheel of your Goddess-Mobile. Enjoy your journey on the Goddess Queen Highroad!

Week One

Meet Your Goddess Queen

This week's Pearls, Activations, Visioning, Prayers, and Stories are designed to introduce you to your inner Goddess Queen. As you remain open and *willing* to explore, you will learn how to contact her at will. This is the beginning of an exciting and transformative excursion into the wondrous being that is you.

Goddess Queen Prayer

With each breath, I drink in the sweet nectar of the Spirit. The sunlight of High Heaven shines upon me, as I find myself, once again, seated at the right hand of Mother/Father God, in a throne that has been custom tailored for me.

From where I sit, in this Heavenly Queendom, I see with X-ray vision, through, above, and beyond the clouds of fear and self-doubt, worry and despair, into the deep abiding love, peace, harmony, and opulence that passes all human understanding, that underlies all things. With this awareness I am no longer fascinated and mesmerized by the foolery and trickery of the worldly illusion of lack and limitation. From this vantage point, I see into the heart of even the seemingly most challenging situations and circumstances, and know, and feel, to the depths of my soul, the love that is always unconditionally there. I know that every ounce of me is filled with beauty, light, love, kindness, nurturing, compassion, mercy, grace, and creative genius; all the ingredients necessary for an immensely successful and fulfilling life. This is my inevitable, unavoidable birthright and true nature. Nothing that has ever happened to me, that I have ever done, or will do, can undo this truth.

As I know this for myself, I simultaneously know and accept this truth on behalf of every being on the planet. All people, places, things, and events, seen and unseen, are conspiring on behalf of my greatest good. All around me darkness turns to light, sadness to joy, despair to hope, lack to abundance; Heaven breaks out everywhere. It is my joy to be the needle that pops a hole in the bubble of illusion, fear, pain and separation!

I sing, dance, frolic, and play in this sanctuary and playground I affectionately call Mother Earth. I join hands with my fellow Goddesses, Queens and Kings and go forth this day with a smile on my lips and a song in my heart; knowing that as I am lifted, all are lifted.

In gratitude for knowing that this is true and has been true since before the beginning of time, I rest these words on the loving wings of Spirit, knowing they do not return unto me void, but fulfilled to overflowing! And so it is. Amen.

Stepping Out

Here I am, stepping into the light.
Here I am, my arms are open wide.
Here I am, stepping into the light,
My arms are open; my heart is open,
I'm not going to fight…anymore.
I feel a celebration, coming over me.
I feel jubilation, for the life given me.
I see it all around me, such blessings everywhere,
It feels like Heaven on earth, it's the answer to my prayer.
That hole in my heart, that always seemed to follow me,
It seemed I'd do most anything, just to find some relief.
But, now I've found the real love, that money just can't buy,
It's bigger than the ocean, takes me higher than the sky.
I'm going out on a limb, arms open, stepping out,
This isn't easy for me; it turns me inside out.
But, if I don't, then surely I will die.
And if I do, I'll have a chance to touch the sky.
Because I'm stepping out, into the light,
I'm willing to love, I will no longer fight.
Here I am, my arms are open wide.
I'm willing to love, I will no longer hide!

Four Questions to Help You Discover

Your Goddess Queen

As you begin this journey, allow these questions to become your mantras: *Who is my Goddess Queen? How do I love her? How do I choose her? How do I listen to her?* As you ask these very important questions, her mysteries will reveal themselves to you. I have found it helpful to carry a journal with me so that I have a place to immediately input my "Goddess Queen 'Aha's" that come in response to these questions.

Question #1: Who Is She?

As I walk this journey, I feel the way I imagine Benjamin Franklin must have felt when he discovered electricity (notice the word "discovered" as opposed to "invented"). He flew his kite in the rain and discovered something that already existed. He didn't "create" electricity; he simply created an *access* to it. While we were living in the dark for centuries, electricity was waiting in the wings for someone to make it *user-friendly!* As I explore, I find that Goddess Queen Consciousness is just like electricity. It has been here all along, waiting just beneath the surface of our clamoring Drama Queen Mind. She waits patiently for us to flip her switch and take advantage of her awesome power.

There are millions of women on the planet, but there is really only one Goddess Queen. Just like there is only one "electricity" that flows into a multitude of unique expressions (lamps, televisions, VCRs, stereos, heaters, air conditioners, etc.). To discover the unique function and qualities of this Goddess Queen that you are, meditate upon the question, "Who is my Goddess Queen?" Remain openly receptive to whatever comes. Feel the empowerment of knowing that all that you need is within you. Owning this knowledge will change your life in the same way electricity changed Benjamin Franklin's life...and the lives of everyone on the planet. By Journaling and Visioning we are flipping the Goddess Queen switch. There is nothing that gives electricity more of a charge—so to speak—than to be used. There is nothing that flips the Goddess Queen Switch more than to be asked for advice. There is nothing that turns her on more than to be invited to dance and explore with you on this mystical journey. There is nothing that would give the Goddess Queen more pleasure than for you to look in your magic mirror and see that she is you!

Question #2: How Do I Love Her?

How do I love her? Let me count the ways...It is a known fact that if you love something, it will reveal its secrets to you. You could say this about a garden, a child, a lover, or a course of study. As you begin to ask the question: *"What is loveable about my Goddess Queen?"* you will be gently guided to see the beauty of your Goddess Queen and appreciate her presence in your own signature way. As you do this, you will become respectful of her and willing to listen to her words of guidance and wisdom. As this takes place, her mysteries and secrets will be revealed to you.

Question #3: How Do I Choose Her?

It is not through martyrdom, heroism, sacrifice or even virtue that one chooses to cultivate a connection to their inner Goddess Queen. This path certainly may appeal to the part of us that wants to lead a *good spiritual life*, but, even the "needy- greedy-survival" part of us (a.k.a. the Drama Queen) can see the benefits of choosing the path of the Goddess Queen. Once upon a time, I used to think of people that were on a "Spiritual Path" as goody two shoes, sugary sweet, and square. A path such as this one never would've appealed to the part of me that is passionately unconventional. But, I now realize that this path is all-inclusive. Every aspect of me is along for the ride.

It used to seem like I was in a tug-of-war with myself. One part of me choosing to take the "high road," while the other part of me would clamor to take the "low road." Upon close investigation, I see that my inner Drama Queen, though sometimes irrationally temperamental, when it comes down to it, only wants peace and to have a sense of security, respect, and love. If I can see past her frenzied crosscurrents of emotion, I can see that my inner Drama Queen is actually quite pragmatic. Even *she* can acknowledge that when she takes the reigns of my life, all hell breaks loose. She can also see that when my Goddess Queen leads the dance, things always turn out in a way that is harmonious and more magnificent than she ever could have planned. From this perspective, I do not need to leave my Drama Queen out of the *choosing* process. In fact, *it is the Drama Queen that this path was created for...she's the one that chooses this road.* She does this easily when she sees that any lesser path will only lead to the heartache, pain and disillusionment that she has already experienced. And when she chooses the path of The Goddess Queen, she can see that she will be led quickly and easily to the realization of her dreams.

When you wake up in the morning, when you go to sleep at night, when you sit down to eat a meal, before you address a challenging situation, before you walk through the door to your job, before you greet your spouse or loved ones...take a moment to become still, take a deep breath, and silently say, *"Goddess Queen that I am, I now choose you to lead me, show me, and guide me. I invoke your presence to take the center stage of my life. I trust you, and I surrender to your wisdom, love, intuition, and guidance."* Allow your own personal Goddess Queen Highroad to reveal itself to you, moment by moment.

Question #4: How do I listen to her?

Take a moment to identify the questions that are circulating throughout your mind and heart: "How am I going to pay for that class?" "Should I call in sick from work today?" "Where is this relationship going?" etc. Write them down in your Goddess Queen Journal. Now set this list aside. Close your eyes, and take a few calming, cleansing breaths. Trace back through your history (or should I say *her* story). Pick one specific moment when you felt on the top of the world; a time when you felt absolutely wonderful about yourself. Where were you? Who were you with? What were you doing? What were you wearing? What time of day or night was it? What did your body feel like? What thoughts were you thinking about yourself? What did you realize about yourself? What feels important to take with you from this peak moment? Allow yourself to viscerally recall the feelings, emotions, and the circumstances of this moment of illumination, until you feel absolutely saturated and filled to overflowing. Now, release the specific circumstances, events, people, places, and things, as you continue marinating in this heightened state. From this place of openness, love, confidence, and connection to your Highest Self, open your journal to the questions you wrote down earlier. Pick up your pen, and allow yourself to write down the answers to your questions. Do not analyze, or judge, just allow wisdom from this heightened state of awareness to fill up the page. Once you have answered the questions, return to your stew of brilliance. Visualize yourself applying the answers. See and feel yourself gracefully applying this mountain top wisdom. Give thanks to your inner Goddess Queen for her guidance. Thank yourself for the courage and boldness that it takes to discover your unique line of Goddess Queen communication!

For the next seven weeks, accumulate other memories of illumination—one at a time, as if you were decorating the Gallery of your Soul with peak moments. As you do this, you may begin to trace certain common denominators among these 'Aha' experiences, certain words, phrases, or directives. Like a detective, place these clues together. Now that you have discovered your very own way of listening to your Goddess Queen, you need never feel powerless, confused, or victimized ever again. If you choose, this can be your defining moment where you cross the line from Drama Queen to Goddess Queen, once and for all!

Pearls of Wisdom
Week One, Meet Your Goddess Queen

The following are your Pearls of Goddess Queen Wisdom for this week. Each day, allow yourself to meditate for ten minutes upon the Goddess Queen pearl of the day. Pay close attention to what the pearl brings up for you and take note of your insights and 'Aha's in the spaces provided.

Day #1: Live today as if it were your last.

Day #2: Cultivate a hunger for transformation.

Day #3: Act as if all of your heart's desires were already fulfilled.

Day #4: Focus more on who you are becoming and less on who you used to be.

Day #5: At every crossroads consult the wisdom of your Goddess Queen.

Day #6: Make your decisions from the place in you that knows you are whole, perfect and complete.

Day #7: Every time you see your reflection in anything, look into your eyes and say, "You are the most gorgeous and amazing Goddess Queen I've ever seen!"

Visioning

Week One, Meet Your Goddess Queen

With heart and mind open wide, for the next 10-20 minutes, enter into the silence, with the intention of releasing any limiting thoughts regarding what you think your Goddess Queen is. To gain a glimpse, an insight, a vision of your highest destiny, begin by asking the questions:

Mother/Father God, what is my highest Goddess Queen self?

What does she look like?

...Feel like?

...Sound like?

...Smell like?

...Act like?

What are her qualities? ...Feeling tone? ...Essence?

What is specifically unique about my Goddess Queen?

What qualities must I cultivate and embody in order to be in harmony with this vision?

What must I release? What must I transform (i.e. habits, patterns, limited ideas)? How can I change in order to be in alignment with my Goddess Queen?

What is the big picture? How does this vision of my Goddess Queen weave into life's grand tapestry? How does my Goddess Queen serve as an integral part of the overall scheme of things?

What is it that I can begin doing right now to honor this vision? What specific, tangible actions can I put into motion right now, to anchor this vision?

Read this to yourself once you are complete with your visioning:

I make a silent, sacred pact with my Creator to honor this grand and Divine vision that has so perfectly and beautifully unfolded before me. I give deep thanks for all that has been revealed, uncovered, uncorked, and made visible. I know that deep in the citadel of my Soul, the highest reality of this vision is already a completed fact, a done deal in the mind of God/Goddess. I wrap this sacred vision in the light of pure awareness. I release it with gratitude unto the law of Spirit, knowing that it does not return unto me void, but fulfilled to overflowing. This or something better, for the highest good of all, is done now. And so it is. Amen!

Activations

Week One, Meet Your Goddess Queen,

The following Activations are designed to bring your Heavenly Visions down to earth. As all of your senses become enlivened, your Goddess Queen is gently nudged from her slumber and invited into the forefront of your awakened life.

1.) *Mirror, Mirror on The Wall:* In your Goddess Queen Journal, write your own Goddess Queen prayer. When you are complete, recite it to yourself, line by line, in the mirror at least once a day.

2.) *Be Scent-sational:* Acquire a new scent that represents your new emerging Goddess Queen Consciousness—perhaps a fragrance that you've never tried…perfume, essential oil, incense, bubble bath, etc. Allow this heavenly aroma to be an *outer demonstration of your inner transformation.*

3.) *If You See It, You Can Be It:* Allow the following question to inspire you to create a Goddess Queen Vision Board: "If I truly invest my heart and soul into this Goddess Queen journey for the next seven weeks, I stand to gain…" On a poster board, glue pictures, words or phrases from magazines that symbolize your Vision and bring it to life. Add glitter, pieces of jewelry, and scraps of fabric, ribbons, and/or feathers. Find a place of honor to display your masterpiece. Spend a few minutes each day of this seven-week journey to view this out-picturing of your Goddess Queen, to reinforce this vision in your heart, mind, body, and soul.

4.) *Goddess Queen Contract:* Sign and date the following contract:

For these next seven weeks, I commit to the following self-nurturing actions:

I commit to Daily Goddess Journaling.

I commit to a weekly Goddess Queen Rendezvous.

I commit to an indulgence in people, places, and activities that support me in cultivating my connection to my Goddess Queen.

I commit to a vacation from people, places, and activities that don't support my Goddess Queen Evolution!

I commit to getting adequate rest.

I commit to daily exercise.

I commit to daily prayer and meditation.

I commit to relating to myself as the Goddess Queen I truly am!

Signature: _____

Today's Date: _____

***

Remember Your Goddess Queen Journaling & Weekly Rendezvous

***

Week Two

The Goddess Queen & Career

This week you will bring your Goddess Queen into the vast terrain of Career; your Life's Work—doing what you love, and loving what you do.

Goddess Queen Divine Career Prayer

As I breathe in the cleansing breath of Spirit, I relax my mind, open my heart, and soften my body. I exhale from all that would dim my light. I unplug my crossed wires of conventional paradigms, mistaken identities, and fearful illusions regarding my unique Career Path. With every new breath, I rewire my system back into Harmony with the Truth of my Being…my Authentic, Passions, Talents, and Desires. I acknowledge that I am an Unrepeatable Phenomenon of Spirit. There is no other being in this world that matches my unique J.O.B. (Joyous Orbit of Bliss) description. As I honor that which "flips my switch" and "turns me on," I am energetically led, step-by-step, moment-by-moment, to the fulfillment of my True Life's Purpose. I am no longer mesmerized by the misconception that in order to be a productive member of society I must work by the sweat of my brow. Struggling upstream is now a distant dream, a thing of the past that no longer carries a charge. I now resonate and vibrate with my Divine Intention for Incarnating in this Dimension. That which I am best at flows as naturally as sunshine warming my face on a bright summer morning. I join hands with my Highest Destiny and I allow my business partner, "The Intrinsic Harmony of the Universe," to guide me gently and gracefully to the Career socket that I am here to plug into. I give thanks for knowing that my Ideal J.O.B. that I was born to fulfill has my name written on it. I am grateful for knowing that my unique contribution to this world is necessary, needed, and indispensable. I know that my Divine Career fills me with electrifying Vitality, exhilarating Aliveness, and an inner and outer Bank Account of Bountiful Bliss. For this I am thankful! In joyous Thanksgiving, I boldly, courageously, and joyously step into the spotlight of my Divine Career, knowing that as I do, I light up the entire world. I release this Truth as I joyously frolic in my Ideal Career/Heaven on Earth, which I know is already complete and fulfilled in Divine Mind. And so it is. Amen.

She Tries

She writes in her diary alone in her bed;
Sorting through the gridlock, piled up in her head.
Another fight with her lover, a bad day for sure
She's looking for some way out, looking for the cure.
'Cause she tries and she cries,
And she smiles when her hearts broken,
Through the years and her fears, her dreams remain unspoken,
In her eyes, in her sighs, you can so clearly see...
How hard she tries.
She feels that she's at the end of her rope,
She's tired of believing, about to give up hope.
She looks up from her diary, and sees a lady in white.
She says, "Please won't you help me out
And show me the light!"
And the lady said, "You don't have to do it all by yourself
Leaving all your angels collecting dust on the shelf...
If you only knew you didn't have to do
Everything all alone
Heaven would rush right in, and carry you home!
Now lift your eyes to the skies
And feel my love with your heart open
Dry your tears, drop your fears,
Let me help, that's all I'm hopin',
In my eyes in my sighs, can you now finally see...
How hard I try?"

Soul Blueprint

I believe that we are born with a Blueprint within us that is absolutely intact—we are whole, perfect, and complete, fulfilled in absolutely every way. As we begin our journey down Life's Path, it is only a matter of time before we get a flat tire, fall into a pothole, slip on an oil spill, or crash head first into a detour sign (i.e. our parents fight, we are slapped, abused, or are witness to some form of abuse, etc.). These are traumatic moments for us. At each of these pivotal situations, it is as if our inner Blueprint gets ripped, and a piece of our soul is "lost." Before long, we get to the point where we feel that we have completely lost all our pieces and we feel inwardly bankrupt. This is the point where we begin to retrace our steps to recapture the Puzzle Pieces of our Soul. The process of re-assembling your inner Puzzle can be greatly quickened when you first remember that *all of the pieces exist*—they haven't disappeared! The truth is that they are all here waiting to be found!

You know when you are bumping up against one of these long lost Pieces when you feel an energetic "YES!" You tingle and become awe struck, with a feeling of aliveness that resounds throughout your entire being. A physical sensation takes you over when you see, feel, or hear something that represents your Soul Blueprint. Some people get chills and for some it is hot flashes (not to be confused with menopause). Your Soul Pieces may come in the form of something you want...a certain quality in yourself...an aspect that you relate to in a lover...best friend...clothing style...business idea...a feeling when you are in a certain environment that just feels "right." Interestingly, what makes your soul *sing*, may make someone else's soul *scream*—it may or may not be something anyone else recognizes as very special. It may be interwoven in the latest fad, or it may be reflected in something that went out of style decades ago.

When we nudge up against one of our precious Soul Pieces, at first we are meant to do nothing more than simply acknowledge it, savor its flavor in our minds and bodies; recognize its essence, and marinate inside of its deliciousness. We do not have to grab, push, pull, or manipulate to get or make our Soul Blueprint come back to life for us.

The Soul Blueprint Mantra is: *"That which is mine cannot pass me by!"* Sometimes our Soul Blueprint reveals itself to us unexpectedly...sometimes long before we are ready (i.e. we will overhear a person talking about their job, one we've always dreamed of—while we are slaving away at a miserable career where we are completely unfulfilled). When this happens the wisest thing to do is to simply acknowledge this as a "Blueprint Moment"—a preview of coming attractions. *Instead of despairing, begin preparing* ...a place for your Soul's Puzzle Pieces to inevitably take shape in your heart, mind, body and soul.

A woman who discovers she is two months pregnant doesn't fret and become hysterical because the baby hasn't made its appearance yet. She knows that this process cannot be rushed. The baby will come when it's good and ready, and not a moment sooner. Ranting and raving is useless, not to mention harmful to the forming of the baby. Instead, she makes the most of this time and begins to prepare herself for the baby's inevitable arrival. She reads "What To Expect When You're Expecting"; she funnels her creative juices into cultivating a beautiful baby room—she prays, meditates, and deepens her Spiritual Life—so that when the baby comes, she is ready.

Apply this Blueprint Perspective to your Goddess Queen Career. As if it was already happening, spend at least five minutes a day this week dwelling inside the energetic vibration of all that flips your Soul Switch. Don't be surprised when you start to see the pieces of your ideal Career synchronistically popping up around every corner!

Quotes for Contemplation

"No matter what your work, let it be your own. No matter what your occupation, let what you are doing be organic. Let it be in your bones. In this way you will open the door by which the affluence of Heaven and Earth shall stream into you." (Emerson).

"When you work, you fulfill a part of earth's furthest dream, assigned to you when that dream was born. And in keeping yourself with labor you are in truth loving life. And to love life through labor is to be intimate with life's inmost secret." (Gibran, *The Prophet*).

"You have a talent that is unique in its expression, so unique that there's no one else alive on this planet that has that talent, or that expression of that talent" (Chopra, *Seven Spiritual Laws of Success*).

The Goddess Queen Time Machine

Close your eyes for five to fifteen minutes and visualize the following:

Imagine you've just stepped foot into a time machine. Notice all the flashing lights, buttons and levers. On the panel to your left, in the lower corner is the dial you can turn to program it to where you want to go. Turn it all the way, as far as it can go, to Goddess Queen Warp Speed. Suddenly the lights go dark...a gust of air sweeps over you...the machine begins to shake and rattle...as smoke billows from the base of this vessel. Then, abruptly, it rumbles to a halt. As the lights resume, you open the latch, and gently push the door open. A very bright light floods your vision as you take your first step outside, into an even brighter light...so bright that it may be difficult to see at first without squinting. When your eyes finally adjust, you begin to notice your surroundings. It begins to dawn on you that you have entered the reality of your Highest Goddess Queen Career. Your senses are saturated with the beauty of this sanctuary—indigo, green, violet, deep reds and blues, yellow, gold, and the sweetest, most luscious fragrance you have ever smelled. If you attempt to think about the things that have been concerning, burdening, or challenging you, you will find it impossible to find them here. In fact, as hard as you search, you will not find your troubles here. Go ahead and look, but, you'll find that your searching is in vain...the harder you look, the more difficult it is to find them...because now they are a distant memory. They've disappeared.

Look around and see that this ideal work environment, your Divine Career is here, before you, now in Technicolor. And like a movie, you hear the music in the background that scores this scene perfectly. As you spend a few moments dwelling in this vision, ask yourself the following questions:

- Who are you when you don't have your troubles or worries to define you?

- How do you feel when your vision is fully realized?

- How do you act?

- How do you walk?

- How do you speak?

- What do you feel inspired to do?

- When you are feeling connected to your Goddess Queen, what kind of work interests or excites you?

- What kind of people do you feel inspired to have around you in your work environment?

- How do they treat you?

- How much money do you make?

- How can you incorporate this vision into your current work situation?

Before you get back into your time machine, take one last look around…take in three deep breaths and imprint this experience into the innermost part of your being. When you feel ready, go ahead and open the latch on your Time Machine. Step inside, and lock the door. Turn the dial that's on the lower left corner, back to today's date. Remember, because you created this experience of your Goddess Queen Career, you can visit it again, any time you wish. Feel the rush of air on your body…feel the shaking and rumbling as the lights flash on. You are now back to home sweet home. Only now, you are more grounded in the awareness of your True North Career than ever before. Spend a few moments daily connecting and embodying the vision of the highest expression of your Divine Career…until it fills you up and effortlessly moves you into your rightful place.

Keep in mind that:

This vision is already a reality in Divine Mind.

All Creation is conspiring on behalf of your greatest and fullest expression!

Pearls of Wisdom
Week Two, The Goddess Queen & Career

The following are your Pearls of Goddess Queen Wisdom for this week. Allow yourself to meditate for ten minutes upon the Goddess Queen Pearl of Wisdom for the day. Pay close attention to what the pearl brings up for you and take note of your insights and 'Aha's in the spaces provided.

Day #8: Honor all of your feelings (all of them) as sacred.

Day #9: Make enough room inside your heart for all aspects of your personality.

Day #10: Imagine your Goddess Queen is beside you all day today. Don't leave home without her!

Day #11: Treat yourself as if you were your own child. Be kind to yourself today when you stumble or fall.

Day #12: Know that when your buttons get pressed you are at your edge; and if you choose you can have a breakthrough.

Day #13: If you are going through a crisis, or a difficult time, remember to keep your attention on the feeling tone of this new, beautiful self you are birthing into.

Day #14: Stand up for yourself if someone's hurtful or inappropriate to you.

Visioning
Week Two, The Goddess Queen & Career

With heart and mind open wide, for the next 10-20 minutes, enter into the silence, with the intention of releasing any limiting thoughts regarding what you think your Goddess Queen Career is. To gain a glimpse, an insight, a vision of your highest destiny, begin by asking the questions:

Mother/Father God, from the highest perspective, what is special about me? What are my unique gifts and talents that I am here to share with this world?

As my Goddess Queen, what is the highest vision of my J.O.B. (Joyous Orbit of Bliss)?

What does it look like?

...Feel like?

...Sound like?

...Smell like?

What are the qualities? ...Feeling tone? ...Essence?

What qualities must I cultivate and embody in order to be in harmony with this vision of my Divine Career?

What is the big picture? How does this vision of my Divine Career weave into life's grand tapestry? How does it serve as an integral part of the overall scheme of things?

What must I release? What must I transform (i.e. habits, patterns, limited ideas)? How must I change in order to be in alignment with my Divine Career?

What is it that I can begin doing right now to honor this vision? What specific, tangible actions can I put into motion right now, to anchor this vision of my Divine Career?

Read this to yourself once you are complete with your visioning:

I make a silent, sacred pact with my Creator to honor this grand vision of my Divine Career that has so perfectly and beautifully unfolded before me. I give deep thanks for all that has been revealed, uncovered, uncorked, and made visible. I know that deep in the citadel of my Soul, the highest reality of my unique Career expression is already a completed fact—a done deal in the mind of God/Goddess. I know that there is a place where my unique talents and gifts are appreciated, needed, and celebrated...I know that this Career provides me with an abundance of energy, acknowledgement, opportunity to contribute, and financial compensation. I wrap this sacred vision in the light of pure awareness, releasing it with gratitude unto the law of Spirit, knowing that it does not return unto me void, but fulfilled to overflowing. This or something better, for the greatest good of all, is done now. And so it is. Amen!

Activations
Week Two, The Goddess Queen & Career

Allow the following Activations to assist you in cultivating the Garden of your Divine Career. Pull out the thoughts or limited ideas that are keeping your true expression underground. Plant some seeds of inspiration and confidence so that your true expression can burst through the soil into fruition. As you do this, you will soon reap the plentiful harvest that comes directly from the fulfillment of your life's Sacred Purpose.

1.) *Out with the Old, and in with the New:* On a sheet of paper, list all of your fears, hurts, resentments, limited beliefs, negative conditioning, and challenging career "issues" from the past. Place this in your kitchen sink, and allow the fire of your passionate desire to burn this to a crisp! As this list burns, feel it burning out of your system, never to return again. Give yourself the gift of a fresh start in your career, starting with a clean Goddess Queen slate.

2.) *A Description Prescription:* In your Goddess Queen Journal, list 20 characteristics that describe the qualities of your Goddess Queen at work. When you are complete, you will have the perfect prescription that describes your real *job* description:

To embody the list
That transforms your career to bliss!

3.) *JOB: Joyous Orbit of Bliss*: Make a list of 100 things that give you joy and bliss. From your neighbor's roses, to the best sex you've ever had. List people, places, things, memories, fantasies, dreams, or successful moments from the past (i.e. winning the award for best drawing in my 5th grade art class, a promotion to manager at my last job, etc.). Make sure you complete your list—don't stop until you've reached 100. Just when you think you can't think of one more thing, keep going. You'll discover that what's on the other side of your momentary block is a treasure trove of buried clues. Once you are complete with your list, with a highlighter pen, underline or take note of any themes, common denominators, or revelations (i.e. shopping, fashion shows, the time I helped Nancy dress up for her big date—hmmmmm, perhaps my J.O.B. is in the fashion industry?). Follow these clues that will lead you to your own unique *Joyous Orbit of Bliss*. When you are attuned to what "turns you on," so to speak, you will be led you to your ideal J.O.B.!

***

Remember Your Goddess Queen
Journaling & Weekly Rendezvous

***

Week Three

The Goddess Queen & Relationship

This week you'll uncover, in the Activations, Visioning, and Stories, ways to mend the places within that have been hurt, and to anchor your Highest Goddess Queen essence into every Relationship in your life...romantic partnerships included!

The Goddess Queen Relationship Prayer

With each breath I take, I release all conditioning and limiting thoughts from my consciousness. I strip away my armor of protection, helmets of limited thinking, my cloak of cynicism, and sword that could injure or wound. I allow myself to be spiritually and emotionally naked as I dive into the lake of Pure Love that resides within me. I swim into the light with the abandon of a child. I know that with my focus on the Divine, I have nothing to fear, nothing to hide, and nothing to blame. I recognize the Unconditional Love, Symmetry, Poetry, and Perfection of this Pool of Grace, Love, and Inseparability with all life that forever saturates me. I recognize that within this Ocean of Devotion, I am never alone...I see, feel, and know that I am connected to the light that interweaves and interconnects all living and loving beings. I know that my life is a continual Marriage Ceremony of God and Goddess. Each day, in every way I am affirming my vows to the Divine that is within me, and the Divine that I see sparkling in the eyes of each precious being I come in contact with. In this Grand Dance of Life, all men, women, and children are my family.

Because of my choice to know the Divine intimately, I affirm and know for myself the Perfect Partner that would swim with me in the deep-end of Intimacy, Love, and Ecstasy. As I remember that only the Love is real, all illusions of fear, separation, doubt, confusion, and fairytale fantasies fall through the drain into the nothingness from whence they came. The Soulful Union between my Divine Partner and I is a place where light and dark...man and woman...adult and child...wounds and healing...Heaven and Earth are joined in Holy Matrimony. I give thanks for this Path of Truth and Enlightenment...for every lesson, challenge, and opportunity to grow and glow into the Radiant Being of Light that I was born to be. Every moment of every day, I am becoming a greater space and a more illumined mirror for the Love, Compassion, Joy, Commitment, and Passion of The Goddess to shine through.

I am grateful for knowing that each step I take upon this Golden Relationship Path is inlaid with treasures. I give thanks for this Alchemy of

Spirit that transforms my frailties to strengths, my doubts to convictions, and my heartache into Rubies of Truth and Wisdom. The Fountain of Love within me overflows with gratitude for being alive and being able to give and share in this Miracle of Love and Union. I release this prayer of Truth unto the law of Spirit, knowing that in the land of Divine Union, the bounty of Perfect Love, Companionship, and Light is already realized in my life. And so it is. Amen.

Twin Flame

I know he's sitting somewhere right now,
But, I don't know where or how.
I'm going to meet this love that Destiny has planned for me.
I can't help but feel that he's so real.
My Twin Flame, I don't even know his name.
A picture without a frame.
But, I'm not afraid of being alone
Because I'm building a home
For my Twin Flame.
I'm getting myself ready for the day,
And living my life every step of the way.
He's not going to pass me by,
My love is shining so bright.
But, I can't deny,
I want him by my side.
My Twin Flame,
I don't even know his name,
I'm a picture without a frame
But, I'm grateful to God, and the Angels above,
Because they're sending me love
From my Twin Flame.

Self-Love

> "When you lack love for yourself, you form an image to cover over the void. That is why being shunned or betrayed in love causes such pain, because the gaping wound of your own need gets exposed." (Chopra, *The Way of the Wizard*).

One night I was out with my girlfriend for her birthday at a nightclub. I met a guy who was particularly interesting and charming (and he spoke Spanish, which used to send my heart into a dither). There was an immediate "click" between us. I noticed him blush when he said I was pretty. That blush catapulted me into a wild fantasy: I imagined that we'd exchange telephone numbers...kiss...go out a few more times...fall in love...get married...have a few children...move to Spain...dance Flamenco...make wild, passionate love 24 hours a day...grow old together...until at last...clenched in each other's loving arms...we'd bid each other, "Vaya Con Dios Mi Amor!"

Then, suddenly, pop, went my little fantasy, when my pouting girlfriend tugged on my sleeve, whining that she wanted to go to another nightclub. Being that it was her birthday, I dutifully accommodated her. Don Juan, very convincingly swore with his sultry eyes that he would meet up with us as soon as he could.

After a couple of hours at the new club, I was getting whiplash from turning my head every five seconds to see if Don Juan had swept through the door. I waited with bated breath, for the grand entrance, right out of "Evita."

Sometimes reality doesn't quite meet up with our fantasies. Yes, you guessed it, the schmuck (do I sound bitter?) never showed. I pretended to be having the most fabulous time, but on the inside I felt nauseous, like I'd just been kicked in the stomach. I was too proud to let my friend know I was devastated. The broken record that kept playing through my mind was: "What did I do wrong?" "Why didn't he show up?" "Was it something I said?" "Or was it something I didn't say?" "Was it my perfume, or lack thereof?" "Maybe my instincts

and intuition aren't as good as I thought." "WHAT'S WRONG WITH ME?"

Suddenly, in the midst of this self-flagellating spiral, something inside me exclaimed, "BULLSHIT!" What surprised me was that it sounded like my Goddess Queen. She doesn't normally yell at me like that; much less use that kind of profanity! It seemed that her angelic voice had become the commanding thunder of an Army Drill Sergeant!

She scolded, "If improving yourself is what you're after, you are barking up the wrong tree! Instead of beating yourself to a pulp, take this window of opportunity to do something useful…Be kind to yourself!"

I replied, "But I don't feel like I deserve any kindness right now! Punishment seems like the only reasonable course of action at a time like this. Obviously, I've done something terribly wrong and bad to cause this guy to reject me. If I punish myself, maybe I'll learn how *not* to do that horrible thing, ever again…if I could only figure out exactly what that horrible thing was?"

"Sounds like a great plan," said my Goddess Queen sarcastically. Then her voice softened with compassion, "Sweetie, if you want to know what that 'horrible thing' was, I'll tell you. You mistook Don Juan for someone outside of yourself that could give you something that you thought you didn't already have. Yes, you gave your power away. You breathed your life force into him. No wonder you're in pain. But, I'm telling you, beating yourself up is only making matters worse. That's like trying to teach precise enunciation to a child with a stuttering problem, by whipping him every time he stammers. Each time you punish yourself, you only deepen your wound of self-loathing even more. Honey, I hate to tell you, but this is counter-productive. You have a choice. You can either spend your energy chastising yourself, or you could take advantage of this priceless opportunity to nurture and love back to health this part of you that feels so raw and exposed. And since this wounded part of you is in plain sight, (actually laying face up on the operating table) it is the perfect time to give yourself the only medicine that will ultimately heal it …Self-Love!"

Her voice then softened even more, "Don Juan gave you a huge gift, which is more valuable than any fling you might have had. He revealed to you your sense of worthlessness. It's time for you to turn within and give yourself the love you were seeking for so desperately outside yourself. Once you are filled with your own love and kindness, not only will you attract a whole new type of man—but you will feel so wonderful about yourself, that he will add to your life, not complete it! Your inner light will be so glowing and infectious, that all you need or want in the relationship department will effortlessly fall at your feet—and the Queendom of Heaven will be yours (well, actually it already is) should you choose to accept it!"

"I accept, I accept!" I exclaimed!

Self-Love Anchor

Take this day to genuinely love yourself. Be kind even to the part of yourself that is unkind. Fast from self-berating and harshness—and instead, soak in all the love, validation, and affection that you've ever wished other people would bestow upon you. Don't be afraid to go overboard; too much Self-Love is never enough. Be ridiculous about it, exaggerate it, go ahead and fall madly in love with yourself. You are gorgeous, admit it; you're priceless, flawless, fabulous. The list is endless. In the wise words of the Goddess Queen, Mae West, "Too much of a good thing…is amazing!"

Tune Her In & Turn Her Up!

So many of us get upset when we can't find the answers to things that we feel are important to know. We feel abandoned by our Higher Wisdom. We whine, "My intuition just doesn't work—and it's not fair!" But, the truth is that it's not your Goddess Queen that is abandoning you; it's *you* that's been abandoning her! This point is illustrated in the following story told to me by my Practitioner, Nirvana:

One summer day, a little girl was playing with her friend. She jumped down some steps, fell, and broke her arm. When her mother asked her:

"Honey, did you consult your wise inner voice before you jumped down those steps?"

The little girl nodded shamefully, "Yes Mommy, I did."

"And she told you to jump?" asked her puzzled mother.

"No, Mommy" she cried. "My wise inner voice told me *not* to jump."

"Then why did you jump?" asked her mother.

The little girl sniffled, then stated matter of factly, "Because the voice of my friend was louder."

Had the Goddess Queen volume been turned up and the static from the outside world tuned out, this little girl could have sidestepped this injury. Cultivating a partnership with your Goddess Queen, and bringing her into your relationships will not only help you avoid falling down the stair steps in life, but will help you to move with graceful accuracy. So, tune in to *Goddess Queen F.M.* (Feminine Mentor) for easy listening on your Soul radio, where you can move to the sound of higher ground, and dance to the beat of your own inner drum. Turn up your intuition—tune out your confusion. Turn up your confidence—tune out your doubts. Turn up your sensitivity—tune out your fear. Turn up your power—tune out your insecurity. As you turn up the volume of your inner radiance, the angelic sound of Romantic Relationship will transmit throughout the heart waves and guide you to True Love and Heaven on Earth!

Wrapping Paper

We look in the mirror—don't like what we see...
A reflection of you, a reflection of me...
The shadow side, the skeleton face,
It doesn't want you to run, it wants to be embraced.
You never wanted to see,
The part of me that was most like me.
My wrapping paper and my bow,
Was all you wanted to know.
There's a part of me that is sometimes scared,
Sometimes fragile, and sometimes bare...
Mysterious, out of control...
There's the fire down in my soul.
I never wanted *you* to see,
The part of me that was most like me.
My wrapping paper and my bow,
Was all *I* wanted you to know.
I need a special man to understand,
One who can love me for all I am.
That kind of man doesn't grow on trees.
Please send him to me, *please!*
I never wanted to see,
The part of *you* that was most like me.
Your wrapping paper and your bow,
Was all I wanted to know.
We look in the mirror—don't like what we see...
A reflection of you, a reflection of me...
The shadow side, the skeleton face,
It doesn't want you to run, it wants to be embraced.
Love me all, not just my pretty side...
For in the dark there are treasures...so come inside.
And I'll do the same for you my love...
And on earth we'll live, in Heaven above!

Openhearted Discernment

One pillar of the Goddess Queen Relationship Temple is "Openhearted Discernment." This is confusing to a lot of women because we tend to either fall into one category or the other. We are either "Openhearted" (innocently trusting and loving), or "Discerning" (cautiously cynical, and protective). How is it possible to combine these opposite qualities? We secretly yearn to love with abandon and feel safe in this world of jagged edges and broken promises. Some of us, regardless of how hurt we've been, continue to be open in the same way as always, thus living in a broken-record of denial and victimization. One reason for this is that when we open up and let our light shine, we become so bright that we attract a great deal of attention. Like the saying goes, "The brighter the light, the bigger the bugs!" This feels so intoxicating that we can overlook the fact that the attention is coming from people that might not be "right" for us. If we lack discernment and aren't stabilized in our power, we move through life blindly and suffer the consequences of falling into many potholes along the way. On the other hand, some of us compensate for our bumps and bruises by posting detour signs around our hearts. Even though life is a lonesome highway when our hearts are closed, we take refuge in our dour attitude because it gives us false security ("At least I'll never fall into that ditch again!") It is clear that living in either extreme is painful. We ask ourselves, "How is it possible to bridge this gap? Is it possible to be openhearted and sensible at the same time? The answer is a resounding YES!

Some of the lessons I've learned in my life have been graceful and effortless. But, it seems my most meaningful lessons have been learned by stumbling from one extreme to the next. The following story is about how I stumbled, fumbled, fell down, and eventually learned about Openhearted Discernment. My hope is that it will serve as a catalyst for you to learn this lesson, perhaps more gracefully than I.

I met a man whose spirituality deeply enchanted me. I was so impressed that I completely discounted the human, personality level reality. Because my "Spiritual" eye was so mesmerized with the grandeur of his Soul, I leapt into relationship with him, while secretly putting a patch over my "Human" eye. It felt so good to throw the doors and windows of my heart open. I lavished my love upon him because that was the experience I wanted to have. *I only wanted to see what I wanted to see.* I judged what my "Human" eye saw as bad ("Oh, Kelly, you're just trying to sabotage the best thing that's ever happened to you because you feel unworthy of being loved. If you were really being the Goddess Queen, you would only see what is wonderful about this guy—his light, love, and kindness. The Goddess Queen would never notice the aspects of him that don't resonate with you—the hairy chest, unkempt apartment, style of dress, hygiene, and the fact that he despises his mother, etc! If you could just patch up that bad "Human" eye long enough, your "Spiritual" eye could take over, and you and he could walk into the sunset together and live happily ever after!")

After I psycho-babbled myself into utter confusion, I learned from our painful yet inevitable break up, that if my goal is to live in Heaven on Earth, then I must honor the perceptions of the unconditional Spiritual eye and the Human personality perception. Both eyes must have the right to cast their vote on what they see.

With this awareness I found myself swinging to the opposite end of the pendulum. When a man would approach me I could feel an invisible barbed wire fence lock in around my heart. My x-ray vision would immediately spot aspects of him (within 30 seconds or less) that I deduced would eventually drive me crazy (a twitch, a mole, a cocky attitude, etc.). This critical perspective worked wonderfully during this self-induced dry spell. However, I was empty and chillingly loveless.

One night while dining with a friend, I had an "Aha Moment." I felt as if a light bulb appeared above my head! I was so excited; it was as if I had just discovered the missing piece of a prized jigsaw puzzle: "Discernment does not have to equal a stone heart, just an *aware heart!*" I was so relieved. I thought, "If I could really do this—keep both of my eyes open, I will naturally see that the Goddess Highroad is paved with the awareness of Spiritual Perfection as well as the acknowledgement of Human Personality. The Goddess Queen weighs and balances both aspects and determines whether or not a person resonates with me. If I walk the Goddess Queen Highroad and keep both eyes open, I will be able to trust myself, which is the key that gives me permission to express the love that is burning in my heart to be expressed!"

Many people, when they commit themselves to a spiritual path, experience such a grand opening in their heart that they literally fall in love with every one they see. They can erroneously interpret this warm rush of sensation as a sign from the universe revealing their "Soul Mate." The truth is, that as we evolve into higher and higher states of illumination, and develop eyes to see the Divine in people, we will be in a constant state of "WOW!" We will fall in love with the bus driver, grocery clerk, the President of the United States, EVERYBODY! This does not mean, however, that we are to have an intimate relationship, or be bosom buddies with them. When you really use your intuition (which works best when your heart is open) you will acknowledge the divine in each person, and relish your wonderful connection, but you will know when it is time to move on...guilt free. Some people you will be led to spend a lifetime with, and others only a few seconds. But whatever it is, it is perfect. I now can clearly see the importance of weaving the Spiritual Perspective together with the Human, the light with the dark, and the "positive" with the "negative." If we do this we can allow our Hearts and Souls to be open wide and we will be led, with discernment to the perfect place, with the perfect people, to the perfect love opportunity, in perfect time, in perfect harmony!

My life is testimony to the fact that Openhearted Discernment is possible. I am now in the most amazing relationship—one that surpasses my wildest dreams—with a man to whom my open heart shouts, "YES!" and both of my eyes give a sparkling wink of approval!

Divine Relationship

May your relationship be
A celebration of passion,
A declaration of love,
A uniting of Souls,
That fits like a glove.
A neon sign of joy,
A billboard made of lights,
A star in the sky,
Pointing to Heavenly heights.
A structure that's large
And that easily bends,
To embrace you in being lovers,
Playmates, and friends...
...King and Queen,
Priest and Priestess,
Committed to support each other's
Highest and best.
May you build your home
In an atmosphere of Peace, Love, and Grace,
Where old illusions and wounds
Can gently erase.
With security and stability
And an unshakable foundation...
To nurture your grandest visions
Into manifestation.

May you bring into the Light,
All of your parts,
As you love one another
With all of your hearts…
With your minds, bodies,
Spirit and Soul,
Mirroring to each other
That you're perfect and whole.
May you be inspired to express
Who you've always been…
Infinite beings
Without beginning or end…
With the freedom and compassion
That only love can bring,
May your hearts be set free,
And may your Souls sing.
As you are carried across the threshold
Of your "Enlightenment Initiation"
And catapulted into a higher vibration
You'll become a vessel,
For God's vision to birth
The Queendom of Heaven…right here on earth!

Pearls of Wisdom
Week Three, The Goddess Queen & Relationship

The following are your Pearls of Goddess Queen Wisdom for this week. Each day, allow yourself to meditate for ten minutes upon the Goddess Queen pearl of the day. Pay close attention to what the pearl brings up for you and take note of your insights and 'Aha's in the spaces provided.

Day #15: Behave as if you were the most loved being on the planet.

Day #16: Know that whether or not they show it, everyone you see loves you.

Day #17: Become a magnet for synchronicities by looking for them and acknowledging them.

Day #18: When in doubt, open your heart and love.

Day #19: Imagine that you have special powers that allow you to see through people's hurts, illusions, and aberrant behavior, into the depths of their radiant magnificence.

Day #20: Be Present. It is the greatest gift you can give yourself or someone you love.

Day #21: Treat every person you see, especially those who challenge you, as if they were your own precious children.

Visioning

Week Three, The Goddess Queen & Relationships

With heart and mind open wide, for the next 10-20 minutes, enter into the silence, with the intention and purpose of releasing any old, limiting thoughts regarding who you think your Goddess Queen is. To open yourself to a glimpse, an insight, a vision of your Highest Destiny with regards to Relationships, begin by asking the question:

Mother/Father God, from the highest perspective, *who* is my Goddess Queen in Relationship?

What does she look like?

...Feel like?

...Sound like?

...Act like?

What are her qualities? ...Feeling tone? ...Essence?

How would my unconditionally loving, Spiritual self integrate with my Human personality in my relationships?

What qualities must I cultivate and embody in order to be in harmony with this vision of my Divine Relationship?

What is the big picture? How does this vision of Relationship weave into life's grand tapestry? How does it serve as an integral part of the overall scheme of things?

What must I release? What must I transform (i.e. habits, patterns, limited ideas)? How must I change in order to be in alignment with my Goddess Queen in the Relationship domain?

What is it that I can begin doing right now to honor this vision? What specific, tangible actions can I put into motion right now, to anchor this vision of my Goddess Queen in Relationship?

Read this to yourself once you are complete with your visioning:

I make a silent, sacred pact with my Creator to honor this grand vision of my Goddess Queen in Relationship that has so perfectly and beautifully unfolded before me. I give deep thanks for all that has been revealed, uncovered, uncorked, and made visible. I know that deep in the citadel of my Soul, the highest reality of my Goddess Queen is completely realized in the mind of the Divine. I wrap this sacred vision in the Light of pure awareness, knowing that as I allow my inner love-light to shine with discernment, I attract loving, respectful, intimate, fulfilling relationships that illuminate the entire world. I release this vision with gratitude unto the law of Spirit, knowing that it does not return unto me void, but fulfilled to overflowing. This or something better, for the greatest good of all, is done now. And so it is. Amen!

Activations
Week Three, The Goddess Queen & Relationships

Walk through your life this week *acting as if* your ideal Relationship Vision was already realized. Notice how powerful, confident, peaceful, happy, and energized you feel. Your Sub-Conscious Mind cannot differentiate between that which is real and that which is vividly imagined. When you step into this vibration you become a harmonic landing place for your Relationship Vision to manifest in your Love Life!

1.) *"Alter" Your Relationships:* Transform a dresser, tabletop, corner, or shelf into your Goddess Queen Relationship Domain. This Relationship Altar will be an outer symbol of your Goddess Queen Interior. As you place power objects, candles, oils, and symbols of the four elements (fire, water, earth, and air), upon your altar, you will be preparing to alter (and *altar*) your Love Life in a powerful way.

2.) *Set Your Love Life On Fire:* Make a Twin Flame Prayer Candle: Write a Relationship prayer and paste it to a 12" glass pillar candle. Decorate your candle with glitter, beads, etc. Place this candle on your Goddess Queen Relationship Altar. Each day this week, light this candle, and recite your prayer silently or out loud. Know that each time you do this, you will become more in sync with your Goddess Queen Relationship Vision.

3.) *Create A Loving Mirror:* Write a list of the past/present relationships that mirror your best self. Imagine these people gathered in a circle with you standing in the center. Sense and feel their love, respect, and admiration showering upon you. As you bask in the glow of this Love Circle write down the qualities that you feel reflecting back to you. Feel the connection to your Goddess Queen Identity become unshakably strong.

Now make a list of the past/present relationships that mirror your Drama Queen. Imagine each person on this list standing before you, seeing you now as the Goddess Queen that you truly are. Face each person, one at a time as you visualize their positive response to your Higher Self. As you stand as Goddess Queen, see them transform into their Higher Selves right before your eyes.

Once you are complete, feel the people in your Love Circle lift you on their shoulders as they victoriously honor you for transforming those important relationships. Each day this week, read this list of qualities that describe your Goddess Queen. As you do this, you will reinforce the qualities of the loving and lovable being you truly are.

***

Remember Your Goddess Queen
Journaling & Weekly Rendezvous

***

Week Four

The Goddess Queen & Creativity

Bringing the Goddess Queen into the sacred space called Creativity, will color, brighten, enliven, and add spice to every area of your life. Authenticity, and the ability to be present are the corner stones of Creativity, and a rich, fulfilling life. Allow this week's Activations and Visioning to unlock the doors and windows of your Heart and Soul—to catapult you into your fullest Creative Expression!

Goddess Queen Creativity Prayer

With each breath that I take, I release my furrowed brow, worry wrinkles, fear freckles, and scowls of seriousness from my Goddess Queen Face. I allow myself to take a plunge in a Spiritual Bubble Bath where all conditioning gets scrubbed away, and *all pain gets washed down the drain.* With each inhale, I dry myself with a warm fuzzy towel of self-love and acceptance. I dress myself in my authentic, multi-colored play clothes. I skip, frolic, hop, and dance in the sunshine, freedom, and joyous delight of being alive. I know that this world is one gigantic Toy Store that has no walls or ceiling. I run down the aisles of my life, intuitively guided by my Imagination to the perfect place, the perfect people, at the perfect time. I recognize that my Innocence and Openhearted Creativity continuously flows just beneath the clouds of adult worry, scurry, and hurry. I know that whenever I choose, I can dip into this infinite well of inspiration that is mine and splash every color of my creative rainbow across the canvas of my life. I know that because my inner "Princess" (or "Tomboy" as the case may be) is the keeper of my Kreative Keys, she has full permission to take my Adult Self by the hand and run the show of my Creative life.

I give thanks for knowing that this world is one beautiful Creation …where I come from is the Womb of Creation…and the blood that runs through my veins is pure Creativity. I am thankful for knowing that there is never a lack of ideas, solutions, inspiration, and possibilities. As I splash and frolic in my Fountain Of Youth that overflows my being, I emerge rejuvenated, refreshed, buoyant, and aburst with Abundant Thanks. I am grateful for knowing that this exhilaration is contagious and it rubs off on everyone I see. I release this Prayer unto the Law of Creation. It is done, it is true, and so I set this prayer free, knowing that in the Mind of the Creator, it is a completed masterpiece, framed and hanging on the walls of the Divine Gallery of Light. And so it is. Amen.

Sweetest Serenade

A herd of wild horses, a bull in a china shop,
A deaf mute who wants to scream,
When you can hear a pin drop.

Troubled waters, no one to understand,
A frightened little girl
In the body of a woman.

How inappropriate; a social faux pas;
With no place to yell, her primal call.

Is it safe to let them know, what's really going on in there?
Or will they run away, leaving you alone and in despair?

Who hurt you so bad? Who said you were wrong?
Who said that you were off key,
When you tried to sing your song?

This world can be so harsh, for one with sensitive skin,
Who's a lover not fighter,
Who shouldn't have to prove anything to win.

Clamoring to survive, in a world that is way too small;
A giraffe among mice
Will always be too tall.

A kind and gentle lamb, in a den of deadly thieves,
Who don't give a damn about her hopes,
Or what her soul believes.

Just pretend it doesn't matter, pretend that you don't care,
Pretend that you just don't notice, that this wound needs repair.

Just sweep it under the carpet, hide it under the rug,
When I ask you what you're feeling,
You say, "Nothing," with a casual shrug.

It's easier to go numb, and pretend you're not that deep,
And take your magic to your grave,
To entertain you in eternal sleep.

But what's the good of that? What a waste of time!
To look for a solution in a trite poetic line!

To whom do you turn? Where do you go?
What can you cling to? Who do you know?

Well, there aren't any accidents,
And God doesn't make mistakes.
One day you'll find your tribe,
Where you'll no longer have to fake.

You'll look in the mirror;
Transformed in the blink of an eye.
From a misplaced ugly duckling,
Into a swan about to fly.

One day you'll find your home,
Where you'll no longer masquerade;
And you'll celebrate your sacred song,
As the Sweetest Serenade!

Wearing Your Soul on Your Sleeve

As the Native Americans say, "We are all on a Sacred Path. Each path must be honored. And, all paths ultimately lead to the same place." The following story is about my sister Shannon, who in my opinion, has been true to her path all of her life, even if it has been "The Road Less Traveled." During her freshman year in High School she clearly danced to the beat of her own drum. She shaved her head, dropped out of school, and spent her time studying Carl Jung, Carlos Castaneda, Lynn V. Andrews, and painting "murals" on the walls of our home. Though many would turn their nose up at her life and deem it "socially unacceptable," I think of it as a unique masterpiece of the Divine.

One Friday night, just three days before she was moving to some remote mountain area, she requested that we go "out on the town" together. We went to an elegantly pretentious Beverly Hills "who's who" nightclub. The beautiful people were present and accounted for. It looked like the perfect backdrop for "L.A. Story, Part Deux." Shannon was such an anomaly at this ego-fest that she seemed to be from a different planet. Unlike every other woman at this club, there was no director that she was trying to schmooze, no pretty-boy actor that she needed to be seen with as a career move, and no sugar daddy that she was trying to seduce. Her agenda was actually no agenda at all. She was there, believe it or not, simply, purely, for the purpose of having a good time (what a concept!)

As the two of us waded through the sea of Rolex watches, Armani suits, Donna Karan micro-mini skirts, and Luis Vitton bags, I could hear the silent conversations taking place between the stylish strangers:

"Don't you know who I am?"

"I just spent the last three hours getting made up so that everyone in the room would gawk at me. Please notice me as I pretend that you don't exist."

"I could make you the next big star in Hollywood!"

Of course Shannon has an ego, but compared to the thick, dark, murky atmosphere of self-importance that hovered like L.A. smog, she seemed like the innocent first breath of a mountain morning. Heads turned to look at her as if she was a custom Lamborghini, parading gracefully through the Barrio of East L.A. No one seemed to notice that her wardrobe mainly consisted of a $5 thrift store fake fur jacket with a rip across the shoulder seam.

We settled on the ledge of a neon fountain. Just as I was admiring my sister's unintentionally tousled ponytail, a French couple approached Shannon and said, "Excuse me, but I have to say that you are the most beautiful and breathtaking woman in the entire club. You are like a diamond in the midst of rhinestones!" The couple was drawn to the authentic glow of my sister's spirit.

This situation inspired me to ask the question: What does being authentic have to do with being creatively expressed? The answer that immediately followed was: "You must be *real*. And in order to be *real*, you must find your own inner rhythm and dance, dance, dance—sing, sing, sing the song of your soul—do, make, and create what moves you…no matter what anybody thinks! All the approval in the world is secondary. Having all the understanding, love, and recognition in the world, is merely icing on the cake…because *the authentic life is the reward itself!*"

When you are authentic, you wear your soul on your sleeve. When your soul is worn on your sleeve, you become a catalyst, a dazzling inspiration for people to embrace their True Selves. My sister, Shannon, is a perfect example of Authentic Soulfulness. May we all dance to the beat of our own drums as we encourage each other to be the Authentic, Creative, Goddess Queen's that we were born to be. May we all have the courage and belief in our own essence to take that bold leap into the Spotlight of our lives!

The Deep End of Your Ocean

Empty your heart
Spill all your guts
Let it all hang out
No 'if's, 'and's, or 'but's.
Take note of all
The treasures you find
Unravel the mysteries
Lodged inside your mind.
Purge your soul
Of held-onto regrets
Wage the world's
Most unreasonable bets.
Free yourself
Of every limited notion
And let your Spirit sail
To the deep end of your ocean!

Transform the Domain of Pain

into the Space of Grace

"Our greatest sorrow in life is not that we don't have enough good to satisfy our needs and desires. Our greatest sorrow is, however, that we don't have what it takes to *contain bliss*. We can't contain Bliss because we can't contain our sorrow. We think we can chase it away, push it away, or manipulate it." (Pierrakos)

I remember the first time I consciously recognized my unwillingness to allow pain to pass through me. I was walking through a bustling crowd at a basketball tournament. I was cheering and flying high on adrenaline along with the rest of the crowd. Out of the blue my body began to tighten around a fear in my stomach and a sadness in my heart. It was as if my body was saying to the pain, *"You're spoiling everything...Just when I was having a good time, you had to show up...I didn't invite you...Go away...You're not welcome here!"* I noticed myself trying to slam the door on this unwelcome, intrusive, party pooper.

As soon as I became aware of what I was doing, I stopped myself in my tracks, took a few deep breaths, and simply allowed myself to "be" with the sorrow. I noticed a jittery feeling in my stomach. It felt steely gray and its voice was a choked cry that stammered, *"I'm terrified. I just don't want to get hurt!"*

I immediately became aware that this discomfort came from the fact that my very first Goddess Queen Gathering was just two days away, and I was feeling apprehensive: "Would anyone show up?" "Am I prepared enough?" "Will they like me?" etc. I recognized a cold familiarity. It was the same feeling that was there on my first day of Kindergarten; I was so excruciatingly shy that I couldn't even raise my hand when the teacher called my name. It was the same feeling that was there when I would hear my parents argue. And it was the same feeling that was there when my favorite dog Poochie was put to sleep.

"Sorrow is a place so seldom related to, and so often related from." (Levine)

I realized that all my life I'd been running from sorrow, but this time I asked my Goddess Queen to step into the center of this pain. I asked for the Higher Perspective. I immediately began to see the Goddess Queen Gathering as being a smashing success; that I was not going to be leading this alone, but, She (my Goddess Queen) would be with me. As my pain began to shift and dissipate, I immediately began to feel relief.

As I reflect on that moment, I can see that all my pain really wanted was to be granted space to be acknowledged and embraced. If I am out of the way, the pain itself passes through rather quickly. But when resistance interferes with its passage, enormous suffering takes place. *"What resists, persists!"* It is only the frantic dance of resistance to being present that creates suffering. If we have the courage and the consciousness to simply see the pain for what it is, and refuse to go to battle with it, it will gently dissolve before our eyes. Pain is simply one shade of color of our inner rainbow. All colors must be embraced and granted space. Remember, the amount of pain that we shut out of our inner Queendom equals the amount of Bliss that we rob ourselves of. If we are to thrive in Goddess Queen Creativity, we must remain present. If we are present, we will be an open vessel for Bliss and the Queendom of Heaven will pour through us. With this awareness, we are available, primed and ready for the Divine to have Its way with us: to dance, sing, paint, and celebrate the blissfulness of being alive!

The next time your old friend "pain" tugs on your heart strings, instead of ignoring and resisting, embrace her. Take her by the hand, and lead her through the *Seven Goddess Queen Steps* out of the *Domain Of Pain* into a *Space Of Grace*:

1. Identify where in your body you feel discomfort.

2. Identify what the color is.

3. Identify the size and shape, and texture of it.

4. Ask the pain what sound it would like to make and/or what does it want to say.

5. How old is this wound?

6. Ask the wound what it wants. For what is it craving/ yearning to express?

7. Bring your Goddess Queen into this space, and ask her what she sees and feels. What wisdom does she want to impart to heal this wound and reveal the truth of this situation?

The Dance of the Goddess Queen

She's a one of a kind,
Mysterious jewel,
Filled with wisdom
She didn't learn in school.
She's wild like a child
And free as a bird,
A wise and gentle elder
Yet a playful little girl.
More vast than the ocean,
More brilliant than the sun,
More colorful than a rainbow;
Reflecting light in everyone.
She'll swirl and twirl you
And spin you about;
She'll brighten and enlighten you
And turn you inside and out.
Your Goddess Queen self
In all of her glory
Dances within you
Wanting you to tell her story.
This Queen inside
Longs to be set free.
I recognize her in you
As you recognize her in me.
Surrender to
Her mystical dance,
And heaven will be yours,
If you just give her a chance!

Pearls of Wisdom
Week Four, The Goddess Queen & Creativity

The following are your Pearls of Goddess Queen Wisdom for this week. Each day, allow yourself to meditate for ten minutes upon the Goddess Queen Pearl of the day. Pay close attention to what the pearl brings up for you and take note of your insights and 'Aha's in the spaces provided.

Day #22: Give your inner child permission to run the show today (let her dress you up, take you out!)

Day #23: Be adventurous. Take a detour down a road you've never traveled.

Day #24: Imagine how you would feel if your greatest challenge or conflict was resolved. Carry this feeling with you throughout your day.

Day #25: Celebrate your unique Goddess Queen Rhythm today by dancing to the beat of your own drum.

Day #26: Delight in your magnificence…Love and appreciate yourself for being an unrepeatable phenomenon of Spirit!

Day #27: Treat each challenge as if it were a BID (a Blessing In Disguise).

Day #28: In the midst of any storm, dive into the center where your creativity and power lives.

Visioning
Week Four, The Goddess Queen & Creativity

With heart and mind open wide, enter into the silence for the next 10-20 minutes. Set your intent on releasing limiting thoughts regarding what you think your Goddess Queen Creativity is. Open yourself to gain a glimpse, an insight; a vision of your highest creative destiny. Begin by asking the question:

Mother/Father God, from the highest perspective, *who* is my Goddess Queen with regards to Creativity?

With her soul worn on her sleeve, what does she look like?

...Feel like?

...Sound like?

...Smell like?

...Act like?

What are her qualities? ...Feeling tone? ...Essence?

As my Goddess Queen, what is my ultimate creative expression?

What qualities must I cultivate and embody in order to be in harmony with this vision of my unique Creativity?

What is the big picture? How does this vision of my unique creative expression weave into life's grand tapestry?

What must I release? What must I transform (i.e. habits, patterns, limited ideas)? How must I change in order to be in alignment with my Goddess Queen Creativity?

What can I begin to do right now to honor this vision? What specific, tangible actions can I put into motion right now, to anchor this vision of my Goddess Queen Creative Expression?

Read this to yourself once you are complete with your visioning:

I make a silent, sacred pact with my Goddess Queen to honor this grand vision of my Goddess Queen Creativity that has so perfectly and beautifully unfolded before me. I give deep thanks for all that has been revealed, uncovered, uncorked, and made visible. I know that deep in the citadel of my Soul, the highest reality of my Goddess Queen Identity is a completed fact—a done deal in the mind of the Divine. I know that my *Creator* and the energy that birthed me into being is pure creativity…in its most profound expression. At my core I know that all the colors of my creative rainbow are gloriously blessed—*there is a place and a space, for my Goddess to express.* I wrap this sacred vision in the light of pure awareness. I release this vision with gratitude unto the law of Spirit, knowing that it does not return unto me void, but fulfilled to overflowing. This or something better, for the greatest good of all, is done now. And so it is. Amen!

Activations
Week Four, The Goddess Queen & Creativity

As you allow yourself to frolic in this playground called Goddess Queen Creativity, you will be surprised at how natural, joyous, and transformational it is. As a Goddess Queen, you are the Creator, the Creation, and the Creativity that fuels the world.

1.) *Dare to Wear Your Soul on Your Sleeve:* Wear clothes, makeup, or a hairstyle that expresses your creative self in ways that you've never dared before—be gaudy, eccentric, blasphemous, sexy, ultra-conservative, Victorian, ridiculous, unsafe, extravagant, fancy, eclectic, colorful, monotone, like your favorite movie star or celebrity. Sometimes the simple act of changing our clothing or hairstyle can stir up secret longings, reconnect us with a long forgotten streak of adventure, or recapture a magical aspect of our Creative Palate that can open us to a new horizon.

2.) *Your Inner Kid: The Keeper of Your Kreative Keys:* Close your eyes and time travel back to one of your favorite childhood memories…a moment where you were completely self-expressed. If this is a challenge for you, just continue to relax and breathe until something emerges. If several memories pop up for you, then pick the one that carries the greatest charge: What were you doing? Who were you with? What time of day was it? What were you wearing? What did you feel like emotionally and physically? What did you think about yourself? Spend a day or at least an afternoon devoted to the whim of your inner kid. From this space, allow her to answer the following questions:

My favorite thing to do is: _____!

Nothing is more important than: _____!

If money was not an issue, I would do _____ all day long!

If I were in charge, I would do _____ for a living!

The only people I want to spend time with are _____!

If only I could _____, my life would be complete!

I want the Goddess Queen to know _____ about me!

I want to do _____ today!

Allow your inner Kid to lead you to your inner Treasure Chest. Remember, She holds the Kreative Keys!

3.) *The Five Minute Miracle Meditation:* Each day this week, close your eyes for five minutes, and take ten deep breaths. Feel a Holy, Sacred Light running from the center of the earth, through the base of your spine all the way up to the crown of your head. Imagine a Sacred gathering of all the Creative People that you most admire. Now imagine your Goddess Queen among them, working together on a creative project—*your current creative project!* Feel the highly charged energy present among all of this genius. Allow yourself to marinate in this atmosphere for at least five minutes. All of the collective genius that exists within your circle of Creative Masters exists within your Heart, Mind, Body and Soul! If you are creatively blocked or stuck in a particular area, pose your questions to this group of Masters and heed their miraculous expert advice!

***

Remember Your Goddess Queen Journaling & Weekly Rendezvous

***

Week Five

The Goddess Queen & Abundance

This week you will cultivate the ability to weave Goddess Queen Abundance Consciousness into your life. You will learn that true abundance is not defined by or confined to the balance in your checking account. True Abundance Consciousness is a matter of Spiritual awareness. As you become aware of your Goddess Queen identity (Queen Midas), you will move out of the *Lack Shack*, and into the *Mansion of Expansion*!

Goddess Queen Abundance Prayer

I know that God/Goddess is all there is; the very substance of all things, each breath, and each activity. I know that the totality of God, of Unconditional Love, of Joy, Peace, Perfection, Harmony, Abundance, and Prosperity is everywhere, all the time...emanating from within me at every moment. The windows, doors, and portals of my heart and soul are wide open to receive all the good that is the Goddess's good pleasure to give me. Any sense of fear, doubt, lack, or worry where money is concerned, evaporates back into the nothingness from whence it came. With Grace and Ease, I recline upon the throne of my true identity...basking in the glow of the Opulence that is mine!

Each and every bill, check, and form of money substance that I spend and receive, is blessed. I know that as I become more conscious, awake, and available for Spirit to work through, the more enriched I become. As I accept this truth, and joyously dance and frolic in the richness of my divine inheritance, I create a space for all beings to be uplifted, awakened, and inspired. How good it is to know that this and more has already been given. And so it is. Amen.

Butterfly Abundance

As the caterpillar becomes the butterfly,
The cocoon of poverty, numbness, vagueness,
And unworthiness of my former self begins to shed.
Revealing shiny, sparkling, silky wings
Of opulent beauty and radiance,
I unleash my inner rainbow
And fly into the lavish heights
Of my Divine Inheritance.
All of my needs are abundantly met.
All the health, wealth, vitality, and love…
The fruition of my creative dreams
Are three-dimensionally realized.
With every beat of my heart,
And every flap of my majestic wings
I become a larger threshold for Heaven
To be realized here on Earth.
I give overflowing thanks,
For this cornucopia of blessings called my life.
In joy and effortless connection to the Divine,
I release this truth unto the law of Spirit,
Knowing it is done. And so it is. Amen

Out of the Lack Shack and

into the Mansion of Expansion

One day as I was walking on the beach, I was feeling anxious while attempting to unravel the confused contents of my mind. I was twisted in a knot, feeling stuck and at a loss as to what to do. I was asking God to show me a way out of my *drama du jour*, when suddenly, a voice popped into my head, "My Father's house has many mansions."

I thought, "Great. That's a lovely biblical quote, but what does it have to do with my current circumstances?"

Then I felt a rush of tingling energy as the 'voice' continued, "My Father's house has many mansions, however, lately you've been living in the Lack Shack. No matter how much you have, it's never enough! You feel as if your life is in peril over very minor things. What a shame that someone who has been given so much has such a poverty mentality. Don't you know that if you wanted to, you could move out of the Lack Shack and into the Mansion of Expansion? Well, you can. So what are you waiting for?"

This ringing resonance filled me with clarity. It must have been God speaking, an Angel, or a Spirit Guide. This was the kind of voice that doesn't mess around. A huge grin appeared upon my face, and I began nodding profusely, like a child being asked if she wanted a golden ticket to Disney Land. The clouds in my mind parted, and I could see my Mansion of Expansion majestically rising out of the Garden Of My Dreams. It was built upon the Holy Ground of Infinite Possibilities...furnished with the desires of my Heart and Soul...lavishly decorated with Grace, Beauty, Love, and Peace. The only glitch was that it was surrounded by a barbed wire fence with a bolted lock at the front entrance. I stood there breathless, just a few feet away, yet I could not enter. Needless to say, I was quite disappointed. Then suddenly the voice commanded, "Well, don't just stand there, get the key!"

I searched desperately in my pocket for the key...to no avail.

"Not that kind of key," the voice scolded, "don't you know that Self-Love is the only key that unlocks the gate to the Garden of Your Dreams?"

I stopped my frenzy, closed my eyes, and stammered, "I'm drawing a blank here. Could you please help me out and show me what there is to love about myself?"

Within moments I found myself weeping right there on the beach, as I was shown that God is not separate from me; in fact, God/Goddess lives inside of me...which means my "Lovability List" goes on for miles. What's not to love? Just as I was relishing this delicious moment, I heard a creeeeeeeeek...The gate slowly nudged open and I tiptoed gingerly into the Garden Of My Dreams. As I approached my Mansion of Expansion, I could feel the vibration of Abundance swelling higher and higher. I felt the physical and emotional sensation of all my needs being met. It was true, that from this place, I literally lacked nothing. Just as I was nestling into the coziness of it all, I heard the voice warmly say, "This is your Mansion of Expansion. This is where you're from. This is where you belong. This is where you are always trying to come back to. *Welcome Home!"*

I refer to this vision often. Whenever I find myself lost in the Lack Shack, I remember that I have the key to my True Residence. Regardless of my circumstances, when I realize that I am One with God, filled with Love, Light, Happiness, Health and Wealth, the physical demonstration always reveals itself. The evidence of this consciousness is not always what I immediately expect—but, I've learned that *realization always precedes manifestation*—everything is unfolding in Divine Time. My Father's house has many mansions, and in my Mansion of Expansion, I am at home!

In Goddess We Trust

"Affluence: An abundant flow; it is not about things at all. When we are consciously centered in the universal flow, we experience inner direction and the unfolding of Creative Activity. Things come too, but prosperity is not just having things. It is the consciousness that attracts the things. The 'Rich Mentality' will not come because of your financial involvements. It must come first out of your steady efforts to know God as your supply. Seek first to get the awareness of the allness of substance." (Butterworth)

In the domain of Prosperity/Abundance, the Spiritual Principle, "It is done unto you as you believe," is made exceptionally apparent. If we believe subjectively that we deserve a large amount of money, then we shall have a large amount of money. If our core belief is that it is more noble and pious to live in poverty, then so shall it be. The Universe responds by corresponding to our dominant beliefs. It is not God/Goddess that is depriving us; it is our beliefs that determine our experience.

Whether we are rolling in the dough, or struggling to make ends meet, "Financial Wounds" can be slow to heal. "Money Issues," like family secrets, are closeted in fear and shame. In order to begin the healing process with regards to Prosperity, we need to bring our Core Beliefs into the light of day. If you do not feel comfortable revealing your Core Abundance Beliefs to another person, then begin by being truthful to yourself. Visioning is a non-threatening, yet powerful way to anchor this new Abundance Consciousness. Within the Visioning Process, you will discover your own unique ways of uprooting your limited subjective beliefs. This makes it possible to plant new seeds that will grow the Garden of your Dreams.

As I begin to scan the Core Beliefs of my inner Drama Queen, I hear her inner dialogue, "Hey, you, Goddess Queen…If you're all you're cracked up to be, then why have we had so much financial drama? You are inconsistent with providing for our needs, and basically, *I don't trust you!*"

The core belief of my Drama Queen is *distrust*. Now that I've discovered this I can deal with her at face value. If I allow the Drama Queen to handle my financial affairs by scurrying, fretting, and hoarding, even she can see that the results are disastrous. So what have I got to lose if I turn things over to my Goddess Queen? I can see from my *her*-story that when I allow my Goddess Queen to be my Abundance

Accountant, I always end up in the overflow. When things have gone awry it has been because my Drama Queen insisted on taking over...big mistake! Distrust of the Goddess Queen is distrust of the Abundance of the universe...clearly preposterous!

From this perspective, it is clear that:

> The only way to financially thrive
> Is to put the Drama Queen in the backseat,
> And let the Goddess Queen drive!

Abundance Affirmation

When I allow the Goddess Queen to manage my financial matters, a calm, warm breeze blows through me, as her gentle voice says: "There is so much good for you here. Release your distrust, relax your body, and quiet your mind. Take the Divine Directives that are laid plainly before you. Follow through on the projects that make your heart sing. Engage yourself in activities that will lead you to greater and greater Inner Wealth. As you do this, you will inspire Wealth Consciousness in many others.

Say to yourself each and every time you spend money:

"There is more where this came from, and I am opening wide to receive and share Divine Opulence. I appreciate Money, Prosperity, and Abundance for being the Master Teacher that it is. I give thanks for my financial situation, exactly as it is now; for all that has led to this moment in my financial *her-story*; as well as for the new Consciousness of Wealth that I am so beautifully moving into. I generously give, and abundantly receive all that life has to offer me. I am a Goddess Queen, heiress to all the fortune and grandeur of Heaven and Earth. My receptivity and generosity with the circulation of money is an act of worship to God/Goddess. I revel in the joy that ebbs and flows easily and effortlessly through and as me. I give thanks for knowing that I am a magnet to the Highest and Best that this world has to offer! And so it is. Amen"

Transferring Commodities

"If we really knew how the laws of Prosperity and Abundance operated we would all be in competition to out *give* each other." (Beckwith)

When I heard Rev. Michael Beckwith speak these words on the Metaphysical Laws of Prosperity, it shifted my Abundance Paradigm. I saw that giving from the overflow supports financial circulation, and opens me to more and more good. I understood that as I expand my level of generosity, the more I widen my capacity to receive. I realized that I am never actually *spending* (implying losing something; being left without something valuable) money, time, or energy. The truth is I am really *transferring* commodities from one account to the next. I never lose anything. I simply create a circulation, an energetic vortex of giving and receiving. Which, by the way, is the definition of Affluence.

Pearls of Wisdom
Week Five, The Goddess Queen & Abundance

The following are your Pearls of Goddess Queen Wisdom for this week. Each day, allow yourself to meditate for ten minutes upon the Goddess Queen Pearl of the day. Pay close attention to what the pearl brings up for you and take note of your insights and 'Aha's in the spaces provided.

Day #29: Explore how you can widen your capacity to love and to be loved.

Day #30: Pay all debts, or at least make arrangements to clear them.

Day #31: Spend today feeling as though you were the wealthiest woman on the planet.

Day #32: As you raise your consciousness, give yourself a raise (up your salary!)

Day #33: Be generous with "I love you's" and mean it!

Day #34: Live from the overflow: Give away ten items that you no longer hold as precious.

Day #35: Imagine that each person you come across today is a King or a Queen in disguise.

Visioning
Week Five, The Goddess Queen & Abundance

With heart and mind open wide, for the next 10-20 minutes, enter into the silence, with the intention of releasing any limiting thoughts regarding what you think your Goddess Queen Abundance is. To gain a glimpse, an insight, a vision of your highest Destiny with regards to Abundance...begin by asking the question:

Mother/Father God, who is my Goddess Queen with regards to Abundance?

What does she look like?

   ...Feel like?

   ...Sound like?

   ...Act like?

What are her qualities? ...Feeling tone? ...Essence?

What is specifically unique about my brand of Goddess Queen Abundance?

What qualities must I cultivate and embody in order to be in harmony with this vision of true Affluence?

What is the big picture? How does this vision of my Goddess Queen bounty weave into life's grand tapestry? How does my Goddess Queen Abundance serve as an integral part of the overall scheme of things?

What must I release? What must I transform (i.e. habits, patterns, limited ideas)? How can I change in order to be in alignment with my true Goddess Queen Abundance?

What is it that I can begin doing right now to honor this vision? What specific, tangible actions can I put into motion right now, to anchor this vision?

Read this to yourself once you are complete with your visioning:

I make a silent, sacred pact with my Creator to honor this grand and Divine Vision that has so perfectly and beautifully unfolded before me. I give deep thanks for all that has been revealed, uncovered, uncorked, and made visible. I know that deep in the citadel of my Soul, the highest reality of my Goddess Queen Abundance is already a completed fact, a done deal in the mind of the Divine. I wrap this Sacred vision in the light of pure Awareness, knowing that the more I avail myself to the Opulence of the universe, the more available I am to be a space of Inspiration and Abundance for all people. I release this vision with gratitude unto the law of Spirit, knowing that it does not return unto me void, but fulfilled to overflowing. This or something better, for the greatest good of all, is done now. And so it is. Amen!

Activations
Week Five, The Goddess Queen & Abundance

This week, contemplate the fact that financial issues are Spiritual issues. The more you connect with the Goddess Queen in all your affairs, you are simultaneously synching up with the Divine Flow of Opulence, Abundance, and Creativity. Remember that not only is it the Divine Plan that we be absolutely fulfilled on every level, but as we seek first the Queendom of Heaven, all will be added unto us. The Goddess Queen translation of that is: When we connect first with the Goddess Queen within, we will realize that we *already have it all!*

1.) *Go for the Burn:* In your Goddess Queen journal, write a list of your negative, limited, Core Beliefs about money or Abundance (i.e. "Wealthy people are uncaring and cold," "If I have a lot of money, I will be less spiritual," etc.). Identify where these beliefs came from (parents, culture, a significant traumatic event from childhood, and so forth). Rip this list out of your journal and place it in your sink, as you set fire to it. As the flames dismember the embers of illusion from your consciousness, breathe deeply, and say out loud:

Burn away,
Far away,
Illusions of old,
That no longer hold,
A place in my Heart, Mind, Body, or Soul.
Affluent Goddess, that I was born to be
Rise now from the ashes and reveal yourself to me!

2.) *Take a Walk on the Abundance Side:* Take a 20-30 minute walk along the ocean, sea, or an affluent neighborhood. As you are walking and observing the beauty and lavishness that surrounds you, imagine that this was your first day here on this earth. Without any prior programming or past experience, imagine that you have been gifted with the ability to begin anew…with a blank slate. What new thoughts and ideas would you want to give yourself regarding money? (i.e. "There is enough to go around," "I am entitled to as much as I desire," "Wealthy people are able to make a positive contribution to this world," "Money is a wonderful vehicle for dreams to be realized," etc.)

3.) *A Frame of Reference:* Write a personal check to yourself for the amount of money that you foresee receiving in your Vision of Abundance (the amount can be a yearly sum, an amount of a check for services rendered—from a company or person that you envision generating revenue from…an amount that you would like to see in your checking or savings account). Decorate a picture frame with glitter, shells, or anything that represents abundance to you. Now place this check in the frame and hang it near your altar.

***

Remember Your Goddess Queen Journaling & Weekly Rendezvous

***

Week Six

The Goddess Queen & Sex

Enter into this week gently, or devour it with all the passion of your heart, soul, mind, and body…As you bridge Sacred Sexuality with Spirituality, your ultimate destination is pure soulful, orgasmic, Goddess Queen Bliss! Could there be a more profound and loaded topic to explore as a Goddess Queen? I think not!

Sacred Sexuality Prayer

As the Fountain of Love that I am bubbles, rises, and pours over onto the earth, the Sacred Sexual Queen that I am lives and reigns supreme. All living and loving creatures, like a magnet, are gathered unto me, as my deep abiding love blankets the entire world. There is no end to the infinite supply of my love, joy, passion, nurturing, vision, and wisdom. Love is my very breath, the beating of my heart, the caress of my touch, the rhythm of my dance, the timbre of my voice, the gentle bat of my eyelashes, and the heat that rises from my flesh. Love is what I am, and all that I am, love is. I am Lover of all, and all beings are my lovers. The infinite power of the spheres surrounds me and abides within me as I swirl, spiral, spin, and dance in the ecstasy of pure orgasmic bliss. The drama, pain and suffering of the flesh has no affect over me. My True Power cannot be taken, stolen, or even voluntarily given away. I am impenetrable—unless I want to be. Regardless of the appearance of wounds, injuries, and arrows I have endured in this parenthesis called human existence, I know that the Real Me has not been touched, hurt, harmed or endangered in any way. For I am more than this body and this body of affairs called my life. I am not of this world. I am here, however, for a short time, to revel in this Human Playground; and while frolicking in the joyous, jubilant game of ecstatic delight called human-hood (or Spiritual Hide and Seek, as the case may be), I remind myself and the other Kings and Queens/Gods and Goddesses, who we really are and where we come from: a world of passion and love making...deep-penetrating moment to moment Soul connection...an audible, visible, edible, sensual celebration of Mother and Father God's profound Love for one another! And so it is. Amen.

Ecstasy Dance

Sometimes I try to put a lid on top of what I feel.
I think I need a reason to be happy, just trying to be "real."
But the answer to the problem lies not in this world's "reality."
It's a feeling always moving through me, that I call ecstasy!
And I live the ecstasy dance!
There's a million and one reasons why I could be depressed.
I could complain all night and day, about why my life's a mess.
But the answer to the problem is found so easily;
Out of the fog I'm living in, and into *ecstasy!*
I live the ecstasy dance!
And it doesn't matter who, thinks I'm acting a fool,
Because they'd rather be struck by lightning,
Than feel the joy, it's too frightening.
So, I live the ecstasy dance!
It's not my birthday; I haven't won any prize;
So what is my excuse?
To shine this smile upon my face,
Simply because I choose?
Well, the answer to the problem, is simple when you see,
There are two paths that you can choose, despair or ecstasy!
Choose the ecstasy dance!
And it doesn't matter why; It's always the perfect time.
Because you know there's no limit to the love you can feel,
When you get down and get real,
It's not out of style
To shine your radiant smile.
It's in your blood to be…
In ecstasy!

Make Love Not War

I once heard Reverend Michael Beckwith speak on the subject of cultivating a "Post-War Consciousness." He suggested that we meditate on the question, "What will our life look like once the war is over (the war between countries, or the war in our own life?)" He spoke of the importance of investigating this concept within our own Souls. This made me realize that if I don't have what it takes to be able to be at peace with Peace (in other words, comfortable within my own skin when there are no fires to be put out, bombs going off, enemies to protect myself from, etc.), then once there really is a truce, I won't know what to do with myself. If Peace hasn't taken root within me, I'll have more anxiety when there's Peace than when all hell is breaking loose!

A former military General once said, with tears of joy in his eyes, reflecting upon his career, "I felt so alive back then—firing off instructions during the heat of battle. Yes, in deed, those were the good ol' days." Not to *general-ize*, but I will—most people feel that their existence is justified and validated when they are slaying some kind of dragon. They feel, at those heated moments, that their life truly has a purpose.

Yes, there are obstacles in life to overcome. Yes, there is adversity. Yes, there are challenges that need to be addressed. Yes, these challenges stretch us far beyond our comfort zones and make us into larger more compassionate human beings. And, yes, there is an actual sense of accomplishment when we've finally won a battle. However, the point is to be aware of the tendency to create another conflict so that we can continue to feel useful because we don't know what to do with ourselves when Peace is finally at hand! Our identity can sometimes be so collapsed into being a "Fire Fighter" that a despairing sense of panic can rise out of a cease-fire. And, in no other area in life is there more fire potential than in the domain of Sex!

As you cultivate more of your Goddess Queen Identity into your sex life, you will begin to notice a significant decrease in the drama. If things begin to look unfamiliar...perhaps longer stretches of harmony where previously there was gunfire...lovemaking like you've only dared to dream becoming realized…a resurrection of passion and love—don't panic! This is a good sign! The work you've been engaged in is paying off! Now is not the time to retreat back to familiar Drama Queen Territory. Rest and recover in the pockets of stillness and bliss. Acclimate yourself to Peace. Soon you will retrain yourself to resonate to life as God/Goddess intended it to be. Starting right now, allow yourself to be more interested in the Peace of Heaven than in anything else. Peace will lead you to an unprecedented mystical, jubilant, realm that will surpass your wildest fantasies.

For five minutes, rest in the following questions:

> What will my life be like when the "war" (i.e. tax season, this fight with my lover, this sexual dry spell, etc.) is over?

> What will my sex life be like when I am living as the Goddess Queen?

> What will this world be like when all people realize their own magnificence and their true Divine nature?

> How much Love/Peace/Ecstasy can I handle?"

How Much Love Can I Handle?

How much love can I handle?
How much love can I take?
How much more can I endure,
Before my fortress breaks?
My cup runneth over,
It's spilling on the floor,
For I have never felt so much love
In my life before.
I'm rising into heaven,
Ascending to higher ground;
In this space,
This Holy place, I am finally found.
I have arrived;
I've won the race,
Everywhere I look,
I see God's face.
It's home sweet home;
I can rest my head,
Unpack by bags
And go to bed.
I'll revisit the dream
From the beginning of time
When I knew I was whole,
So pure and sublime.
How much love can I handle?
How much love can I take?
How much more can I endure,
Before my fortress breaks?

Cleaning Your Goddess Queen Pool

A swimming pool, at first glance, may appear to be relatively clean. But once you sweep the bottom of the pool, and bring all the debris to the surface, it appears messier than before. The payoff for all this hard work is that now it can easily be skimmed away, so that you can enjoy a nice, refreshing swim in a cool, clean pool.

When you set an intention to bring your Goddess Queen into your sex life, everything unlike itself must first come up to the surface. Taboos, secrets, shame, and buried pain rise to the top of your sexual pool.

One of the most powerful ways to "clean your pool" is through recording and paying attention to your nighttime dreams. Your dreams are the bridge from your Conscious Mind (12% of your mind's power), to your Sub-Conscious Mind (88% of your mind's power). Your dreams are magical experiences that help you weave and integrate lost pieces of your Soul that your Conscious Mind cannot access. Even if you have a difficult time remembering your dreams at first, that's OK. Set an intention to remember and make the commitment to write down your dreams in your Goddess Queen Journal. Fragments, thoughts, images, or feelings are all noteworthy.

Shortly after setting the intention to bring my Goddess Queen into my sex life, I had the following dream:

I was at a gathering where there was a heavy, somber feeling in the air, as if someone had died. The house was filled with the cacophony of chatty conversations and the clanging of food being served on fine china. I found myself in the kitchen playing with Isabella, my best friend's two-year old daughter. I was thoroughly enjoying myself, watching her go through the full gamut of emotions that babies go through. She was playing and laughing one second, then crying the next, pouting, then, laughing again, and on and on. I was so mesmerized and fascinated by her rainbow of expressions that it did not even dawn on me to discourage her from being too loud, or to insist that she behave like a "perfect little lady." I was in heaven simply enjoying her just as she was. Suddenly I heard the loud, angry footsteps of a man thundering toward the kitchen. Immediately my body became a clenched fist of terror as he shouted, "SHUT HER UP! I DON'T WANT TO HEAR ANOTHER SOUND OUT OF HER!" He was screaming so ferociously, it looked as if a blood vessel would burst.

I froze in my tracks, unable to think or move. Isabella could feel my fear, and began to wail uncontrollably. The man commanded, "GOD DAMN IT, PUT PLASTIC OVER HER HEAD, AND SHOVE HER IN A DRAWER. I DON'T WANT TO HEAR ANY MORE NOISE OUT OF HER!" In my numbness and terror, I did exactly as he instructed. I got out the Saran Wrap, and covered Isabella in it. I poked a little hole where her mouth was so she could breathe. And then I placed her tiny body into a very small silverware drawer, closed it, and stood there frozen. There was a woman washing dishes, so I went over to join her. She tried to make small talk about the lovely wallpaper, as I tried to immerse myself in washing the dishes. As hard as I tried, I couldn't escape the image in my mind of Isabella suffocating in that drawer. I thought to myself, "If she somehow survives this, her self-worth will suffer for the rest of her life. She'll believe that it is not OK to be herself, fully expressed. She'll grow up suppressing her magical self…like me…only pastels and pinks…smiles, and giggles…dead." Then, suddenly, a surge of clarity came over me. I said out loud, with conviction, "I WILL NOT ALLOW THIS CRIME TO HAPPEN TO HER LIKE IT DID TO ME!" I marched over to the silverware drawer, and pulled Isabella out. She was still breathing—barely. I quickly unwrapped her, as she began to cry at the top of her lungs. I held her, as I ran out the door, screaming, "JUST LET HIM TRY AND STOP ME!"

What I learned from that dream was that each character symbolically represented different aspects of my unconscious sexual self: (Isabella) the passionate, out of control little girl with a rainbow of color, emotions, and flavors; (me) the naive and dutiful girl who just wants to please; (the woman) the part of me that's in denial, the part that wants to ignore the pain and talk about wallpaper; (the man) the part of me that desperately wants to control me; (and, of course my Goddess Queen who came to the rescue) the part that is awake and committed to protecting me from anyone who might attempt to harm or suppress my sexuality in any way—including myself.

It has been said, "You cannot heal what you cannot feel." Not only did I feel the fear, but I woke up with my pillow drenched in tears. Within this cathartic dream I found the courage to move out of this unhealthy box I had been living in. Because of this dream, not only did I discover my weakness, but I found my strength. I have since been able to weave my Goddess Queen into my sexuality, to heal and transmute my inner critic and numbness, to make room for my passion, and full sexual expression.

Remember, that in order to bring the bounty of your Goddess Queen Sexuality to the forefront of your life, you must purify the pain, shame, and blame from your inner pool. My hope is that you will allow your dreams (your inner pool man) to expedite the recovery of your lost parts that have been awaiting you at the bottom of your pool. In so doing, you will be able to go skinny-dipping in your Goddess Queen Sexuality and enjoy all the ecstasy that is in store for you!

Goddess Is My Name

Nothing to hide.
Nothing to blame.
I've cleaned out my closet,
Relinquished my shame.
My passion and desires
I need no longer tame.
I unleash my true essence;
From the rooftops I proclaim,
"My sacred sexuality
I finally reclaim.
I ascend from the ashes
And Goddess is my name!"

The Goddess Queen 'IntimaC's

By embodying the Goddess Queen 'IntimaC's: Connection, Communication, Compassion, and Creativity, sex can become a tool that will liberate, expand, and awaken you and your mate to who you really are...One with God.

Connection is the ability and gift of ecstatic surrendering to the Wholeness of Life, Love, and your partner's Body, Mind, Heart, and Soul. When you can release that which keeps you feeling separate, you will merge back to the Source of Oneness, Wholeness, and Unification with all life.

Prayer and Visioning are tools that my partner and I have found useful to bring us back to a state of union.

Communication is the ability to express the nuances and depths of how you intimately feel, what you want and need. It is the ability to listen to and receive the verbal and non-verbal messages of your sexual partner.

My partner and I find that the more we know about each other's likes, dislikes, and even past sexual experiences the closer we feel and the more our love expands.

Compassion is the ability to read between the lines and feel energetically, physically, and emotionally what your partner is feeling, wanting, and needing. It is the psychic sensitivity that allows you to be graceful and appropriate to the delicacy and tenderness of the moment.

At times, my partner and I energetically slip into each other's skin while making love. When we allow ourselves to have this powerful experience, our level of sensitivity rises, and our appreciation and love for each other always increases.

Creativity comes from an innate sense of safety that will give you and your partner the wings to experiment with new and spontaneous ways to make love. Feeling free to be adventurous and inspired in the moment will allow the Goddess Queen within you to boldly lead you into uncharted terrain.

For some of us, the Goddess Queen 'IntimaC's are difficult because we were not raised to honor our bodies or cherish our sexuality. Because we don't believe that our fundamental sexual drives and desires are healthy and beautiful, it makes sense that we would be out of touch with our sexual rhythms and instincts. However, the moment that we realize our Sexuality is Sacred, the healing process begins. As a Goddess Queen, you no longer have the luxury of being a victim. In order to uncoil from the darkness of this tunnel and emerge into the Light, you must have a sincere, and specific intent to bring your Highest Self to Sexuality. Learn to cultivate your Goddess Queen Vision—*what you can see, you can be.* If you are in a relationship, invite your partner to share your vision. As a Goddess Queen, it is your charge to fully realize that your sexuality is a precious gift to you, your mate, and to this world. Your Goddess Queen Consciousness will alter the entire trajectory of your sexual relationship path and your life. If you truly embody the *Goddess Queen 'IntimaC's: Connection, Communication, Compassion, and Creativity* you will be initiated into the realm of Sacred Sexuality: a co-creation of Heaven on Earth; a reuniting of Souls; a spontaneous miracle of Enlightenment; and an ever-deepening expansion of Love!

Pearls of Wisdom
Week Six, The Goddess Queen & Sex

The following are your Pearls of Goddess Queen Wisdom for this week. Each day, allow yourself to meditate for ten minutes upon the Goddess Queen Pearl of the day. Pay close attention to what the pearl brings up for you and take note of your insights and 'Aha's in the spaces provided.

Day #36: Say, "Yes!" to adventure, opportunities, and invitations.

Day #37: Add something sexy or Goddess-like to your wardrobe.

Day #38: Express your Goddess Queen *Scent*-suality: Wear your favorite perfume for no particular reason.

Day #39: Wear a scarf or some flowing fabric and dance around your house to your favorite music.

Day #40: Dip into sensuality with a Goddess Queen Bath. Add candles, incense, soft music, and privacy.

Day #41: Live today from your "G-spot" (Goddess spot)…as if you knew that you were the most desirable woman in the world.

Day #42: Write yourself a love letter and praise yourself lavishly for being Goddess's gift to this world!

Visioning
Week Six, The Goddess Queen & Sex

With heart and mind open wide, for the next 10-20 minutes, enter into the silence, with the intention of releasing any limiting thoughts regarding what you think your Goddess Queen Sexuality is. To gain a glimpse, an insight, a vision of your highest destiny with regards to Sacred Sexuality...begin by asking the question:

Mother/Father God, who is my highest Goddess Queen Sexual Self?

What does she look like?

　...Feel like?

　...Sound like?

　...Act like?

What are her qualities? ...Feeling tone? ...Essence?

What is specifically unique about my Goddess Queen Sexuality?

How can I embody the Goddess Queen 'IntimaC's (*Connection, Communication, Compassion, and Creativity)* into my life?

What is the big picture? How does this vision of my highest Goddess Queen Sexuality weave into life's grand tapestry? How does my Goddess Queen Sexual Energy serve as an integral part in the overall scheme of things?

What must I clean out from the bottom of my Sexual Pool? What must I transform (i.e. habits, patterns, limited ideas)? How can I change in order to be in alignment with my Goddess Queen Sexuality?

What can I begin to do right now to honor this Vision? What specific, tangible actions can I put into motion right now, to anchor this Vision?

Read this to yourself once you are complete with your visioning:

I make a silent, sacred pact with my Creator to honor this grand and Divine Vision that has so perfectly and beautifully unfolded before me. I give deep thanks for all that has been revealed, uncovered, uncorked, and made visible. I know that deep in the citadel of my Soul, the highest reality of my Goddess Queen Sexuality is fully realized. I know that my Sexuality is a gift from Heaven for me and to this world. I wrap this sacred Vision in the light of pure awareness, releasing it with gratitude unto the law of Spirit, knowing that it does not return unto me void, but fulfilled to overflowing. This or something better, for the greatest good of all, is done now. And so it is. Amen!

Activations

Week Six, The Goddess Queen & Sex

To the degree that you show up as the Goddess Queen is the degree to which your relationship, sexual or otherwise, will improve. Whether or not your partner is open to exploring this terrain with you, if *you* are open and adventurous enough to experiment with these suggestions, then there will be magic, unexpected delight, and surprising bursts of ecstasy in store for you!

1.) *Erect Your Self-esteem:* If your libido has gone limp, take heart. There are many ways to bring blood back into the areas of your majestic inner Queendom. Create a sacred, silent atmosphere for yourself, complete with candles and soft music. Close your eyes and visualize or feel Goddess light and heat, perhaps the color red (passion), tingling its way through your toes...up your legs...into your pelvic area...womb...up your spine...into your breasts...down your arms...into your fingers...into your neck...face...lips...and crown Chakra. Imagine that you are being massaged, and/or kissed from head to toe by God/Goddess/Love itself. Allow this delight to spill over into your lovemaking. Add a splash of: perfume, lingerie, make-up, and heels to add a little extra spice to your bedroom repertoire. Remember, that the more you incorporate into your life that which feeds your self-esteem, the more your Sexual Power will rise and bestow Its lavish gifts upon you and your mate!

2.) *Pray Your Way to Ecstasy:* Prayer opens the gateway to the mystical and magical. Within the realm of prayer is a bridge that can transport you from being identified with your hurts, wounds, resentments, and unfulfilled expectations into a land of unity, bliss, fusion, and ecstasy. Praying while making love can be done in silence or out loud, depending upon the receptivity of your partner. When the Goddess makes love to her partner, or to herself, she remembers she is making love to pure Divinity in the flesh. Affirm your connection to Spirit with each stroke, kiss, and touch.

3.) *If your "Turn on" button has been "turned off":* Turn on your favorite sensual music...a song that flips the switch of your inner aliveness. Either alone or in the presence of your lover, allow the Goddess Queen within you to move your body in her own unique sensually expressive way. Allow yourself to escape into a mystical reverie of beauty, rapture, heat, and the orgasmic joy of being alive.

4.) *Copy the following affirmation; declare it daily with exclamation:*

I am ecstasy giving birth.
Because of me, Heaven is realized on Earth.
I inspire people to be their best
By living my life with passion and zest!
I am a fountain of God's direction and love,
My Goddess Queen Sexuality fits me like a glove.
Every day
In every way
I am fulfilling my intention
For incarnating in this dimension!

***

Remember Your Goddess Queen
Journaling & Weekly Rendezvous

***

Week Seven

The Goddess Queen & Having It All

No doubt, you've begun to notice some changes in your life. That's because you've been moving for these past six weeks from one house to another...out of the *Lack Shack* and into the *Mansion of Expansion.* You've been packing boxes...discarding what you no longer need...dusting off that which you love, cherish, and want to keep...acquiring a few essential articles that will help to turn your *Mansion of Expansion* into *Home Sweet Home.*

This week is about reaping the rewards of all your hard work and honoring how far you've come. You can now stand tall and proud despite the occasional challenge (which at this point, you welcome as an opportunity to develop your Goddess Queen Consciousness even more). The most difficult part is behind you. Relax, let go, and enjoy the rest of what life has to offer you. Remember that as you continue to cultivate this Goddess Queen Consciousness, you create a space for all men, women, and children to do the same! Celebrate! Applaud yourself! Enjoy and revel in your success, Goddess Queen!

Goddess Queen Having It All Prayer

I take this moment to acknowledge and embrace how far I have come on this journey of discovering and cultivating a relationship with my Goddess Queen. I have covered vast inner territory...scaled high mountains...trudged through the valley of the shadow of death...and allowed my Spirit to free-fall with newfound trust into the loving arms of Spirit. I've flown, soared, climbed, crawled, danced, sung, played, frolicked, cried, wept, laughed, and rejoiced. Never let it be said that I haven't truly lived! In all my excavating I've created more room for the preciousness of my Spirit to shine more freely and unencumbered than ever before. My love burns brighter than it ever has. My wisdom speaks more clearly to me than ever before. My ability to see through illusion has never been sharper. My ability to surrender to the Love that surrounds me has never been greater. My ability to listen and pick up the cues that the Universe is always sending me has never been more accurate. My life is truly on course, and I, at this exact moment, am exactly where I am supposed to be. I truly am a Queen of the highest order...a Goddess of the deepest dimensions. I sit now on my Royal Throne and lovingly accept the blessings that are mine. How good it is to know that as I do this, I am a reminder to all others that they too are magnificent. I am truly grateful for this Awareness, and to know that, as good as this is, this is only the beginning. In an outpouring of thanksgiving, I release this word, and allow it to be. Knowing it is done; and has been since before the beginning of time. And so it is. Amen

I'm Free

I'm up, I'm down,
I'm side to side.
I feel I'm on
A wild ride.
I don't know
The reason why
I hurt so bad.
Sometimes I want to die;
And a simple kiss
Sends me to bliss.
The Truth is
I am more than this.
I turn within,
Drop down to the well,
Know the Truth,
That all is well.
I'm the beginning, I'm the end.
I'm a lover, I'm a friend.
I am woman, I am man.
I am footprints in the sand.
I'm eternity,
I am Free!

The Circle of Elders

When I first tapped into Goddess Queen Awareness, I noticed a shift taking place within. I went from being identified primarily with "Student Consciousness" to "Teacher Consciousness." "Student Consciousness" is a dependence upon a source of wisdom outside of Self. "Teacher Consciousness" is primarily characterized by a recognition that the source of all knowledge, wisdom, and illumination lies within. The springboard for this transformation revealed itself to me during a particularly profound meditation.

I saw my Goddess Queen Self upon a mountaintop, seated at a round table with: Jesus, Mother Teresa, Ghandi, Martin Luther King Jr., and Mary Magdalene. My life was the subject of discussion. Jesus leaned over to me, gave me a gentle nudge, and whispered in my ear. My Goddess Queen listened attentively and nodded. She responded, "Thank you so much. I'll take your advice into consideration. Your wisdom is quite profound. However, I feel inspired to take a different route than the one you suggested."

I was flabbergasted! My Goddess Queen just edited Jesus! And she did so without arrogance, apologies, or rebellion; but simply because she was in touch with what was Highest and Best for her.

Jesus gestured with a respectful and approving nod. He then proceeded to ask her advice on some issues that he was processing! At different times during this Summit meeting, my Goddess Queen would be asked for her advice and perspective on the different issues. She would also receive bursts of wisdom transmitted through the other sages. There was a synergistic give and take, and by the end of the meeting, all members were elevated to new heights of Illumination. They all agreed to reconvene very soon; since they were all just a "meditation away!"

When I came back down to earth, I was brimming with a profound sense of inner strength. Realizing that I am connected to the Source of Illumination, I felt inspired to implement this new way of interacting with people. I learned that I do not need to defend what I know, or try to cram my awareness down someone else's throat. Instead, I can gently filter that which feels appropriate to receive and appropriate to share. I can now receive insights from others without abandoning my own inner wisdom. In other words, being anchored in my powerful Goddess Queen identity transformed my fragile uncertainty into quiet strength.

Circle of Elders Meditation

From the ultimate state of consciousness, there is only One Mind throughout all time and space. By the power of thought, we can literally bond with the wisdom of Jesus, Buddha, Gandhi, Mary Magdalene, Mother Theresa and Krishna. We do this by simply directing our thought and intention to the place in consciousness where they reside.

When two or more are gathered, the Power and Presence of God is realized...but, when there is a summit meeting such as this, God/Goddess Consciousness is transported to new and greater heights.

For 10-20 minutes, sit in the stillness, and allow your breathing to become deep, gentle, and rhythmic. Envision yourself seated at a Round Table with brilliant minds, enlightened souls, and loving hearts. See yourself as the Goddess Queen that you are, in all of your power, wisdom, and glory. Sense and feel that you are a respected peer among these fully actualized beings. Feel your inner light growing brighter and brighter as you are rising and expanding your vibration to the level of this collective light. As you connect to this heightened state of awareness, feel this vibration move through every cell of your physical being, from your toes, to the top of your head. Allow any unanswered questions you have to be brought to the table for discussion. Feel your quiet strength gently guide you to receive and share the answers that come to you.

Return to this meditation anytime you are confused, uncertain, or at a crossroads in your life.

On a Warm August Eve

Escorted onto the lawn on a warm August night
Into an embrace of love that was too strong to fight.
Tingling chills danced up my spine,
As my kindreds became anointed with lavender wine.
Cleansing me, bathing me, of all my false thoughts,
Of any need for my armor or fortress of locks.
My pettiness and self-doubt crumbled away
My knees nearly buckled when they began to pray.
A whimsical breeze took flight in my hair,
As I surrendered and connected to the angels gathered there.
On a gilded throne I was told to please take my seat,
As they adorned me with stars on my head and my feet.
They each held a candle that cast their faces aglow,
Illumining the soul mates I've personally come to know.
One by one they approached me, speaking in their own unique way
Of the specialness of our connection that their sparkling eyes did convey.
They told me they were honored and touched by my light
That I had in some way helped their souls to take flight.
What a blessing to be present, alive, and aware
To behold all of this love, showering upon me in my chair.
Like a sponge, I did my best to soak up every drop
Of this heavenly moment I did not want to stop.
I believe that each one belongs in the center of this wheel
To abide in the love I had the grace that night to feel.
That ceremony will be with me all throughout my years
I'll never forget you…you magnificent mirrors.
Time will not erase what is now etched deep in my heart,
This love that was shared, I know is only the start.
A legacy of love for my great-grandchildren I will leave,
Tales of illumination from that warm August eve.

Having It All

I was getting a haircut from my girlfriend, Nicole. We were chatting about our lives, (like girlfriends do when we get our hair done). We were talking about all the compromises we have to make in life. I was speaking from an "Either/Or Consciousness," about the high price tag on all the "good things in life." I felt the cost of having something I wanted meant that I had to give up something else that I wanted.

Nicole asked me, "What would happen to you if you believed that you could really have it all? What would you envision your life to be?"

As I began to contemplate this question, I took a deep breath, and suddenly felt my spirit lifting, as a rosy glow flushed across my face. I answered, "I would want to be with a man who is spiritual, but down to earth. I also want to be with someone who is passionately in love with me, who can also give me my space when I need it. I want to have a flexible career that pays an excellent income, where I only work when I feel like it. I want to have a family, kids, friends, a booming business, and all the time I want to take time to smell the roses, to take vacations, to write," etc. I could've gone on and on.

Nicole, in all of her Goddess Queen authority, responded, "You can have whatever you want. If you say that you have to make compromises and 'go without', then so shall it be. But, if you say, it is your birthright to have it all, then so shall it be. Kelly, *you can have it all!*"

Not only did I leave Ruby Begonia Hair Studio that day with a fabulous, bouncy new haircut...but, I left with the realization, *"I can have it all!"*

I know that life is a constant balancing act, and sometimes in the three-dimensional world, things do not always *appear* as if I am having it all. However, the Goddess Queen Consciousness transcends the physical reality. We know as Goddess Queens that the unseen world is more real than the visible world of effects. If we vibrate with the consciousness of having all aspects of our lives thriving at maximum potential, and we take the corresponding action that this vision dictates, it will be just a matter of time before "Having It All" becomes physicalized in our lives.

Having It All Affirmations

The universe *responds* to my dominant beliefs

As a Goddess Queen it is my birthright to *have it all*!

As I realize the "Having it all" Consciousness, it is now becoming *physicalized*!

Heaven's Playground

There's a place I go
When I close my eyes,
The shore of Shangri-La,
Next door to Paradise.
The people there
Don't mess around,
Fussing and fighting
Putting each other down.
They've got one life,
They're of one mind,
They're all one for each other,
In this place and time.
Harmony, serenity abound…
In Heaven's Playground.
There's a place I go
When you hold me close,
From the top of my head,
Down to my toes.
Loving you…
There's no end in sight.
Dancing in ecstasy,
Day and night.

We've got one life,
We're of one mind,
All one for each other,
In this place and time.
Harmony, serenity abound...
In Heaven's Playground.
It doesn't matter how we get there
And it's OK to make mistakes.
Just as long as we get there,
No matter what it takes.
Heaven's Playground
Is the place to be,
Heaven's Playground
Is for you and me.
Heaven's Playground
Let your Soul be free.
Heaven's Playground,
Lives inside of you and me!

Pearls of Wisdom
Week Seven, The Goddess Queen & Having It All

The following are your Pearls of Goddess Queen Wisdom for this week. Allow yourself to meditate for ten minutes upon the Goddess Queen Pearl of the day. Pay close attention to what the pearl brings up for you and take note of your insights and 'Aha's in the spaces provided.

Day #43: Tie up all loose ends (i.e. if applicable, make apologies, or arrangements to pay off any debts, or complete unfinished business).

Day #44: Give yourself permission to make mistakes today and record them in your journal.

Day #45: Apply the wisdom you learned from your "mistakes" yesterday.

Day #46: Allow, "I can have it all" to be your mantra today.

Day #47: Extend your love and service to another person today as a demonstration of the loving and generous Goddess Queen that you are.

Day #48: Make a Self-appreciation list of all the things you've discovered about yourself over the past seven weeks.

Day #49: Acknowledge three people today for the positive contribution they've made to your life over these seven weeks.

Pearl for the Rest of Your Life

Day #50: Let your light shine. Remember that the more you radiate, the brighter your world becomes!

Visioning

Week Seven, The Goddess Queen & Having It All

With heart and mind open wide, for the next 10-20 minutes, enter into the silence, with the intention of releasing any limiting thoughts about who you think your Goddess Queen is. To gain a glimpse, an insight, a vision of your highest destiny with regards to having it all in your Career, Relationships, Creativity, Abundance, and Sex life...begin by asking the questions:

Mother/Father God, as I embrace the fact that I truly already have it all, who is my Goddess Queen?

What does she look like?

...Feel like?

...Sound like?

...Smell like?

...Act like?

What are her qualities? ...Feeling tone? ...Essence?

What is specifically unique about my Goddess Queen?

What qualities must I cultivate and embody in order to be in harmony with this vision of having it all (all of the various areas of my life, career, relationship, creativity, money, and sex, etc.)?

What is the big picture? How does this vision of my Goddess Queen weave into life's grand tapestry? How does my Goddess Queen serve as an integral part of the overall scheme of things?

What must I release? What must I transform (i.e. habits, patterns, limited ideas)? How can I change in order to be in alignment with my Goddess Queen in all the various areas of my life?

What is it that I can begin doing right now to honor this vision? What specific, tangible actions can I put into motion right now, to anchor this vision of my Goddess Queen into my every day life, in every way, everyday?

Read this to yourself once you are complete with your visioning:

I make a silent, sacred pact with my Creator to honor this grand and Divine vision that has so perfectly and beautifully unfolded before me. I give deep thanks for all that has been revealed, uncovered, uncorked, and made visible. I know that deep in the citadel of my Soul, the highest reality of my Goddess Queen—who has it all, is already a completed fact, a done deal in the mind of God/Goddess. I wrap this Sacred Vision of all areas of my life thriving in the light of pure awareness, releasing it with gratitude unto the law of Spirit, knowing that it does not return unto me void, but fulfilled to overflowing. This or something better, for the greatest good of all, is done now. And so it is. Amen!

Activations

Week Seven, The Goddess Queen & Having It All

As you are traveling along the Goddess Queen Highroad, it is important to stop, from time to time, to take a breath, acknowledge the view, and pat yourself on the back for the progress you've made. The Goddess Queen knows that she is hot stuff...that she is a dazzling, amazing, masterpiece of love, beauty, and compassion. It is wise to take some time to appreciate your progress, courage, change, growth, and transformation. This can be an enormously empowering and important task. When your inner Drama Queen can see tangible evidence of Goddess Queen Consciousness paying off in her life, she becomes more willing to cooperate and continue along this path of Transformation. Remember that there is no "end" to this journey, no final destination—no end to Light, Love, and Ecstasy. However, this is the appointed time to rest your knapsacks, and take stock of your milestones.

1.) *Stick to it:* Go to a craft store and purchase a packet of stickers (stars, hearts, etc.). Read through your Goddess Queen Journal and Workbook. Revisit your journaling, visioning, and dreams. Place a sticker next to any themes, patterns, or 'Aha's that you have gleaned as a result of undergoing this Goddess Queen journey.

2.) *A purse full of GEM's:* (**G**oddess **E**nlightenment **M**anifesting) As you go through your Goddess Queen Journal and Workbook, pull out a separate sheet of paper, entitled:

"Goddess Queen Gems: Insights and Divine Directives"

List the *GEM's* that you have accumulated, in other words, the places in your Journal and Workbook that you have placed stickers. For example, if you placed a sticker in your journal that says, "*I really want to take a dance class*," then write, "*take a dance class*" on your list. If there is a sticker next to a place that you wrote, "*I really hate being an accountant; I'd much rather be a clothing designer*" then write, "*buy a sketchpad for design ideas*." Write down the specific insights and action steps that will support you in anchoring these Goddess Queen Insights. Keep this list of GEM's readily accessible in your purse, so that you can refer to it many times throughout the day.

3.) *A Date with Destiny:* Write a date next to the items on your List of GEM's that mark the projected fulfillment of your tasks and insights. Release any sense of pressure or resistance. Create this date with the spirit of joyous anticipation. As you fulfill each GEM on your list, check it off, and give yourself a Goddess Queen Reward (i.e. a trip to your favorite day spa, that dress you've been dreaming about buying, an afternoon of R&R, etc.). If the GEM does not become realized by the date that you set, then simply cross it out, and create a new date. Do all that you can to fulfill this intention. This simple process of creating a "Date with Destiny" is one way that the Goddess Queen grounds Heaven to Earth!

4.) *Goddess Queen Life Design:* Leaf through several magazines, and tear out different pictures, words, or images that represent your Goddess Queen Having It All. Paste, glue, or tape your beautiful images on a poster board. In the center of your Life Design, write your own Goddess Queen prayer or affirmation. Display this masterpiece in a place of honor. Refer to it often as you continue along the Goddess Queen Highroad!

Afterword

I want to take this time to acknowledge you and express my gratitude to you for honoring your inner Wise Woman and the courage it has taken for you to embark upon this "Goddess Queen" excursion! I feel enormously grateful for having had the privilege and blessed opportunity to travel this journey with you. Because of your willingness to grow (because we are all connected), you/I/we have all been uplifted. I know that you are not the same woman reading this that you were seven weeks ago! I acknowledge you for your growth, learning, sharing, laughter, generosity, openness, and most of all the depth of Spirit that you've brought to this expedition. I am so honored to be in such company. Know that I am, and will always be, in your corner, cheering you on.

Thank you for the blessings you have added to my life, and to the lives of so many others. Thank you for being the bright, beautiful star that you are. May the wings of your Heart and Soul continue to stay open so that you may fly higher and higher on the winds of Unconditional Love; touching and inspiring many as you journey deeper and deeper into the Truth of your Spirit. My prayers are eternally with you. I look forward to our paths intertwining again as our inner rhythms move us to the Divine beat of the Goddess Queen!

Peace & Blessings,
Kelly

Guidelines for a Goddess Queen Gathering

The main reason I wrote this book was to empower women throughout the world to live from their Goddess Queen Center. I realized that the best way to manifest this vision would be to establish a format for woman to facilitate their own Goddess Queen Gatherings. So, if you feel inspired to share in this vision and help to perpetuate the Goddess Queen Consciousness, then YIPEE! I tip my crown to you. The following are some suggestions to support you in being a "Space Holder" for your own Goddess Queen Gathering:

Discuss with the group that the success of your Goddess Queen Gathering is entirely up to the level of participation and commitment of each woman. The Gathering can be a womb of profound transformation.

This group is a microcosm of how you interact in the world, and in your relationships. You can use this group as a laboratory, a place to experiment with being a Goddess Queen in your ideal relationship; one in which there is communication, closeness, depth, intimacy, sharing, caring, and honesty. Each woman is unique in her own way and this group can be something that directly addresses her particular issues.

One way to empower the success of your Goddess Queen Gathering is through honest, deep, soulful *communication!* I cannot emphasize the importance of this enough. Each group is in its own way like an intimate relationship, in that at a certain point, the entire spectrum of feelings will arise. Anticipate these emotions ahead of time as an inevitable part of any deep, meaningful relationship. So, when the going gets tough, rocky, and uncomfortable, you acknowledge that, like sand in the oyster, a beautiful pearl is being formed.

Every participant in your group is intuitive and psychic to varying degrees. But, most of us are so absorbed in our own lives that we don't tune in to other people's custom designed needs, wants, and desires. A "No Withholds Policy" is strongly advised. Sometimes the most challenging interchanges, when dealt with compassionate honesty lead to the most rewarding breakthroughs. Remember that Goddess Queens communicate until a resolution has taken place.

Metaphysically speaking, that which is known somewhere in consciousness, is simultaneously known everywhere. In this way, the Higher Vision of the Goddess Queen Gathering is to inspire, transform, and uplift the Spirit and Consciousness for all people...one woman at a time. As one is lifted, all are lifted.

Notes about Goddess Queen Gatherings

- Gatherings can last between 2-4 hours.
- A Goddess Queen Gathering is best hosted in a space that is quiet and private.
- Each person is seen as sacred, whole, perfect, and complete.
- Time should be allotted for each woman to share her progress, challenges, and victories.
- This is a supportive group, where receiving and sharing are of equal importance.
- Confidentiality is a must.
- Honor the time. Begin and end promptly, according to the designated times. I suggest that each woman, when sharing, be mindful of the time, so that everyone will have a chance to participate.

Note for "The Space Holder"

Remain flexible and present with the specific needs and desires of your group. Remember, the guidelines are here to serve as a helpful blueprint, but nothing is set in stone. The highest needs of the group are always first and foremost. With your intuition as a guide, feel free to add your own spice and creativity.

Format for a Goddess Queen Gathering

1.) *Releasing Ceremony:*
Pass a candle around the circle. Each woman says, "I, (name), now give to the flame _____ (anything that is keeping you from being present, i.e. bills, a fight with husband, stress from the drive, etc.)." Once each woman has had a chance to give her cares and concerns to the flame, then the last person blows out the candle.

2.) *Embracing Ceremony:*
The Space Holder provides a "talking stick" (i.e. a wand, or sacred, power object). Each woman will take a turn holding the stick as she says aloud the quality that she wants to embrace during the course of the gathering. For example, "I, (Kelly), embrace the quality of (peace, love, joy, or abundance, etc.)."

3.) *Opening Prayer:*
You can either play *"The Goddess Queen Gathering"* CD, or the Space Holder can say her own opening prayer. For example:

"I evoke the power of the Great Goddess Queen that resides within. I align myself with her Peace, Clarity, and Unconditional love. From this place of authority, I claim Wholeness, Perfection, and Oneness with the Goddess Queen for every one here. From this place of united Power, Purpose, and Passion, I call forth the intention for this Gathering. I claim this to be a space of Transformation, Integration, Illumination, and Inspiration. I claim this to be a time of Awakening to our True Nature. I give thanks in advance for knowing that this gathering unfolds perfectly, and that it uplifts us all to be the Goddess Queens that we were born to be…for the Highest Good of all. I release this unto the law of Spirit. And so it is. Amen."

4.) *Purpose Statement*:
The Goddess Queen Gathering is: A space of Transformation, Integration, Illumination and connection to the highest, wisest, most loving, powerful aspect of ourselves. By meeting on a weekly basis we build our Goddess Queen Muscles, so that our inner Wise Woman can take the reins of our lives, and lead us into our highest potential...as women, lovers, mothers, friends, and leaders. As we are lifted, all are lifted!

5.) *Intention:*
Five minutes of silence in which each woman contemplates her intention (what she'd like to gain from being in the group ultimately, as well as what she'd like to get out of being there that particular day).

6.) *Introduction:*
While passing the talking stick from person to person, each woman shares her purpose and intent.

7.) *Visioning:*
You can either listen to "The Goddess Queen Visioning CD," or the Space Holder can read the Visioning for the corresponding week out of this Workbook.

8.) *Sharing The Vision:*
Each woman passes the "talking stick" and shares her insights from the Visioning.

9.) *Quality:*
Each woman will take turns sharing with the group the quality she has chosen to cultivate that week. (i.e. self- love, nurturing, joy, bliss, peace, stillness, confidence, strength, acceptance, prosperity, etc...). This quality is something that you court, carry around with you, explore, bring into your meditation, and daily thoughts.

10.) *Accountability:*
A weekly Accountability is something you commit to do between meetings that will assist you in developing your Goddess Queen Consciousness (i.e. a yoga class, a walk on the beach, a creative project, meditating, buying flowers, taking a bubble bath, etc.). It will be unique for each person. It should have specific, measurable results. An "Accountability" is something that would not ordinarily take place during the normal course of your schedule. Every week there will be a check-in where each person reports their experience with their weekly "Accountability."

11.) *Prayer Partners:*
This is a partnering between two women from the group, for the duration of the class. Either the Space Holder will assign prayer partners, or will draw names out of a hat. Prayer partners should arrange a time to connect at a certain point outside of class each week, either on the phone or in person. As a prayer partner, you pray for your partner and see her in her highest light. Based upon what the particular needs are, prayer partners can be moral support, a sounding board, a baby sitter, or simply a loving space of prayer each week.

12.) *Debrief:*
Before closing for the evening, the Space Holder should go through the Goddess Queen Weekly Check-list:

- Accountability & Quality
- Goddess Queen Rendezvous
- Journaling (2-3 pages a day, including nighttime dreams and a gratitude list)
- Pearls Of Wisdom
- Activations (outlined at the end of each week)
- Connecting with Goddess Queen Prayer Partner

13.) *Closing Prayer:*
You can either listen to "The Goddess Queen Visioning CD" or the Space Holder can say her own closing prayer. For example:

"*We give thanks* for all that has unfolded during this Goddess Queen Gathering. We acknowledge all the Miracles, Insights, and Revelations. We soak into our cells and into the marrow of our bones the Light and Love and Empowerment that we feel right now. We carry this with us as we leave here. We consciously infuse this energy into all aspects of our lives, as we commit to ourselves, and to each other, to live from this day forward as the Goddess Queens; the Lights of the world that we were born to be. We give thanks for the participation of each one of us tonight. We are all blessed as we leave here. We give thanks for knowing that as we have been lifted, all beings are lifted. Thank Goddess for this precious gathering. And so it is. Amen."

References

Beckwith, Rev. Dr. Michael (Agape Church of Religious Science).

Butterworth, Eric. *Spiritual Economics. The Principles & Process of True Prosperity.* Unity School of Christianity, 2001.

Chopra, Deepak. *Seven Spiritual Laws of Success.* Amber-Allen Publishing, 1995.

Chopra, Deepak. *The Way of the Wizard: Twenty Spiritual Lessons in Creating the Life You Want.* Crown Publishing Group, 1996.

de Sosa, Ruth; Fire Star; Sullivan, Kelly. *Goddess in a Pinch.*

Emerson, Ralph Waldo.

Gibran, Kahlil. *The Prophet.* Alfred A. Knopf Incorporated, 1977.

Goethe.

Levine, Steven and Ondrea. *Embracing the Beloved: Relationship As a Path of Awakening.* Anchor Books, 1996.

Gayle, Nirvana.

Pierrakos, Eva. *The Pathwork of Self-Transformation.* Bantam-Doubleday Dell, 1990.

Smith, Professor Huston.

Steinem, Gloria. *Goddesses in Everywoman: A New Psychology of Women.* Foreword. First Harper Colophon, 1985.

Walsh, Neil Donald. *Conversations with God.* Putnam Publishing Group, 1996.

Williamson, Marrianne. *A Woman's Worth.* Ballantine Books, 1994.